BRAD *Leading Man*
Pitt

Sophie Lees

ICON
PRESS

© 2005 by Icon Press
First printed in 2005 10 9 8 7 6 5 4 3 2 1
Printed in Canada

The Publisher: Icon Press is an imprint of Folklore Publishing
Website: www.folklorepublishing.com

Library and Archives Canada Cataloguing in Publication

Lees, Sophie, 1970–
  Brad Pitt : reluctant leading man / Sophie Lees.

(Star biographies)
Includes bibliographical references.
ISBN 1-894864-44-1

  1. Pitt, Brad, 1963– 2. Motion picture actors and actresses—United States—Biography. I. Title. II. Series.

PN2287.P55L43 2005   791.4302'8'092   C2005-902136-5

Project Director: Faye Boer
Project Editor: Élan Publications Management
Production & Layout: Trina Koscielnuk
Cover: Valentino, Burch Zahary
Book Design: Anne Iles & Dion Moon
Cover Image: Courtesy of International Communications Systems

Photography credits: Every effort has been made to accurately credit the sources of photographs. Any errors or omissions should be directed to the publisher for changes in future editions. Photographs courtesy of International Communications Systems.

We acknowledge the support of the Alberta Foundation for the Arts for our publishing program.

PC:P6

Table
of
Contents

Introduction 6

Chapter 1: Growing Up Brad 10

Chapter 2: Brother Pitt Goes to College 18

Chapter 3: Go West, Young Man 26

Chapter 4: Taking Off 36

Chapter 5: Learning to Fly 50

Chapter 6: Of Legends and Vampires 64

Chapter 7: Playing House 78

Chapter 8: Climbing Mountains 90

Chapter 9: A Charlie Brown Year 100

Chapter 10: Back on Top 112

Chapter 11: Looking Ahead 126

Filmography 136

Notes on Sources 140

★ ★ ★

Dedication

To my fellow Brad watcher, Ben.

Acknowledgments

I want to thank the people who run the Brad Pitt Center website—www.pittcenter.com—whose hard work and dedication have created an incredible resource for any and all things Brad. I encourage Brad Pitt fans to check it out. I'd also like to thank my editor Lisa Pashniak for her contribution to the book.

Introduction

Since he sauntered onscreen as JD in *Thelma and Louise,* stealing both Thelma's heart and her savings, Brad Pitt has been unstoppable. Leading roles in *A River Runs Through It, Interview with a Vampire* and *Legends of the Fall* cemented his status as his generation's screen stud. He was hailed as the new James Dean, who was a gorgeous, but troubled, young man. Brad scoffed at the comparison, wondering why anyone would want to be like a tragic icon that died too young. Throughout his career, Brad has fought against being seen as the next James Dean, the next Robert Redford, the next Steve McQueen or, indeed, the next *anyone.* He has been determined to carve a place for himself as far as possible from the position Hollywood wanted for him, that of "golden boy" and later, the handsome leading man. Brad has always wanted more—he's wanted to be a good actor.

I first saw Brad Pitt in *Thelma and Louise* and was immediately struck by his screen presence. I stayed to watch the credits so I could find out his name. I've seen every one of his films since. The truth is, I find Brad fascinating, and not because of his good looks but for many other reasons including the variety of roles he chooses. I've never been able to label him. Every time I see one of his films, he surprises me. And for me, surprise is too often missing in Hollywood movies. He is, indeed, a breath of fresh air.

Brad is also a seriously good-looking guy. Tall, lean, with a natural six-pack, Brad has a body men spend hours at the gym to achieve and other people simply dream about. He's also blessed with an angelic face: full lips, high cheekbones, electric blue eyes and a smile

> ...Brad has been determined to be true to himself and to his values.

that makes women's hearts beat faster. Supposedly even better looking in person, Brad is certainly eye-candy on screen. But at times, he has found his looks frustrating because people don't see beyond them, and Brad has more to offer than his pretty face. As he matures, he is becoming an accomplished actor. It's been said that Brad is a character actor trapped in a leading actor's body, and that may be true. His best work has been when he has played character parts or when he is part of a talented ensemble.

No one would question Brad's position as an A-list actor, commanding $17.5 million per film. And yet, to date, Brad has not been a big box office draw—not like Tom Cruise or Julia Roberts who guarantee the studios a big opening weekend. Brad is much more hit-and-miss. Many of his films are not blockbuster material, but Brad has also starred in some big movies that have flopped big-time at the box office. So, how does he continue to be such hot property when he isn't making millions for the studios?

The truth is, Brad is movie star, and we'll love him no matter what—we just may not go to every film he does. We love him because when we see him up on the screen, we can sense he is the real thing, a genuine person. Throughout his career, Brad has been determined to be true to himself and to his values. So far, largely successful, that determination has strengthened his personal qualities of genuineness, honesty, courage, and adventurousness, all of which make him more appealing to us on screen. Box office success or not, Hollywood seems as taken with Brad as the rest of us.

And it seems that we can't get enough of him; his every move-ment is recorded for a public hungry for information about his private life. We want to know Brad, the real Brad, and not just the characters he plays. His characters have touched us, perhaps in ways we've never been touched, and we want more. Now with technology such as the Internet and telephoto lenses, we can see into his private life quite easily. Tabloids feed on our desire for information, and we buy them even if the information they give us is mostly lies. But at what cost to Brad and the other celebrities involved?

> Brad has become fiercely private; he rarely does television appearances and interviews and, when he does sit down with the press, he doesn't like to talk about his life outside of his movies. He lives isolated from the public. In fact, other than his family, he hangs out almost exclusively with other celebrities, like his good friends, couple Catherine Keener and Dermot Mulroney.

Even before he was star, Brad appeared in the tabloids. He landed in print courtesy of Robin Givens, whom he began dating after filming an episode of *Head of the Class*. At the time, Robin was in the process of breaking up with her now ex-husband, Mike Tyson, and her liaison with a pretty boy like Brad was too juicy for the tabloids not to exploit. Since then, tabloids have been vigilant in reporting every real and imagined aspect of Brad's love life. And it's not just the tabloids, but also the mainstream press who have followed his three main romances: Juliette Lewis, Gwyneth Paltrow and Jennifer Aniston. With each of his loves, we've witnessed Brad madly in love, declaring his feelings to the world, and then heartbroken and withdrawn after the relation-ships have soured.

So, who is Brad Pitt—voted twice as *People's* Sexiest Man of the Year? Everyone who has worked with him likes him; he is described as cool, considerate, charming, down-to-earth, unspoiled by his fame. He is remarkably intelligent, well read, and fascinated by architecture. Brad has been blessed with, not only his stunning physical beauty and easy charm, but also his family who provided unconditional love, guidance, and security. And over the almost twenty years of living in Hollywood, Brad has grown from a 22-year-old boy, seeking to find himself, to a 41-year-old man, who is settling into himself.

But even with all he's been given, Brad has a lot to deal with, mainly in the romance department. After seven years together and four and one-half years of marriage, Brad and Jen, the golden Hollywood couple, are no more. The family Brad is so eager to start will have to wait a little longer.

For me and for plenty of other people, Brad is simply fascinating. Even though he may look like an angel, he seems to be just so *human.*

growing up
Brad

G rowing up, I always judged things according to how I would behave in that situation, and I was a naive kid because I really believed....I've just come to understand that people don't think like I do.

William Bradley Pitt was born on December 18, 1963, in Shawnee, Oklahoma. Named after his father, Bill Pitt, Brad was called by his middle name to avoid confusion. Brad was the first child of Bill, a manager of a trucking company and Jane, a high-school counselor and homemaker. After his birth the family left for Springfield, Missouri. Other than Brad, who left Springfield to follow his dream, the Pitt family hasn't moved since. Now with their own families, Brad's younger brother Doug and sister Julie still call Springfield home.

Little wonder the Pitts have settled there. According to the Employment Review, Springfield is listed in its *America's Ten Best Places to Live and Work* publication. Calling Springfield "the cultural center of the Ozarks," the review commends the city's "thriving economy, first rate education and superior health care." Brad is still attached to Springfield, and his relationship with his family remains close. As soon as he could, he purchased 600 acres for himself and his family in the Ozark Mountains plateau, where Springfield is nestled. Brad often spends time there: "I get back there maybe three times a year. We live out in the woods, on the river. It's peaceful there...I can appreciate the life there now that I've left it." Brad has always sought refuge in nature. As a child, needing nothing more than his imagination and the outdoors, he spent hours playing in the woods behind his house, located on the outskirts of Springfield.

Missouri is part of the Midwest, a distinct cultural grouping. Culturally, Midwesterners haven't forgotten their pioneer roots: the men here keep their emotions tucked away, and people are respectful of folks' privacy. They don't go around talking about problems or their feelings. Much of Brad's public persona is attributed to his growing up in the Midwest, particularly his dislike of talking about himself and his reserve onscreen. Brad himself supports this idea: "Where I grew up, you deal. You get through it, power through it, straight up the middle. And you don't complain." Midwesterners are also characterized as being open, friendly, and straightforward, three qualities that Brad epitomizes.

Missouri's influence on Brad goes even deeper. The state is also part of the Bible Belt, a group of southern and midwestern states noted for their religious fundamentalism. But Brad is not known for his religious fundamentalism, certainly not now, and while growing up, he struggled with his family's religion. His parents were strict Baptists, attending church every week and observing its teachings. Brad has said that who he is today comes from his childhood and religion: "Everything stems from growing up Baptist." His family's religion was the main source of discomfort for Brad as a child, though he is thankful now for the experience, because "it kept my mind on bigger things." But going to church was tortuous. While there, he wished he could make some startling loud noise and then "stand up and yell, 'It was me! Right here!'" Perhaps he hoped to get kicked out before the end of the sermon, when "the preacher would pick someone to read the final prayer, and I would go into

"The truth is, I don't want people to know me. I don't know a thing about my favorite actors. I don't think you should. They become personalities."

a sweat, afraid he would pick me. I would sit there and say, 'Please, God, not me.' That was my final prayer."

Besides church, Brad's childhood, by all accounts, was healthy and happy—two loving, supportive parents and two younger, worshipping siblings. Not poor, not rich, both parents worked hard to provide their children with a sense of comfort and well-being. Sister Julie recalls, "I always looked up to both my brothers. I just thought they were the greatest. Doug and Brad really played off each other. We just had such a close family, and I think that gave us confidence."

Another glimpse of the Pitt family comes from Chris Shudy, one of Pitt's college friends, who observed, "Brad looks like his father, and he has the personality of his mother. His mother is so down to earth, just a super woman. His dad's a great guy, but more reserved. *A River Runs Through It* is almost a mirror of Brad's family. When I saw the movie, I called him and said, 'You're not even acting, it's just your home unit minus Julie.'"

Brad himself tells the most about his parents and his childhood; he has called them "the biggest guides in my life." The influence of both his parents can be clearly seen in his choices even now.

In an interview with Diane Sawyer, Brad described his father as "integrity. He's very unassuming, but he walks…he just walks it. You feel it. And where we grew up, it was all about actions and not words. We didn't have much of a vocabulary. It was just actions." Bill's philosophy made an indelible impression on Brad, who believes the same. When he is in an interview, however, it can frustrate Brad and journalists because he can't understand why people want to hear what he has to say on any given topic. An actor's worth is about action, about the characters he plays. "The truth is, I don't want people to know me. I don't know a thing about my favorite actors. I don't think you should. They become personalities."

Brad is particularly fond of recalling one story about his father. As a young teenager, Brad was playing a heated game of tennis. He lost his temper, and flinging his racquet down, he had a full-blown tantrum. Bill came up to him after the game. "He just said, 'Are you having fun?' I got all huffy and said, 'No.' He looked at me and said, 'Then don't do it,' and walked away. Boy, that put me in my place. I should have gotten my ass kicked, but he was so above that." It was huge lesson for Brad; he took it to heart, and it still informs his decisions today.

Whereas his relationship with his father was etched in actions, his relationship with his mother was about words. As for his mother, Brad described her to Diane Sawyer as "goodness. A lovely, lovely woman. Growing up, we would, you know, we would have our bedtimes. And so the three of us siblings, we'd jump in our beds, separate rooms, and we'd all be yelling for her, because she'd take turns coming from room to room, right? And we'd just talk for hours sometimes. Just talk."

In those talks with his mother, Brad was able to figure out many things. As a child, he had already developed a remarkable awareness of the larger picture, realizing that the world stretched far beyond his own life. He'd even begun to understand that he was not just good-looking but extraordinarily so, and his looks gave him advantages. It worried him, and so he talked to his mom. "I was painfully aware of some doors opening where they didn't for others. And I would ask my mother. My mom would come to our rooms when we were little and talk us to sleep. We'd talk for a half-hour. And I remember asking her about this at a very young age, like, 'why isn't the world fair?' And she would say to me that it's not, but this means that you have more responsibility. And it's something that's always rung in my head. How you handle it. What you do with it."

His mother's answer confirmed a truth many parents would turn away from: good looks have extraordinary value in our society, and they do open doors. But she also spoke to Brad's ethical nature and offered guidance in coping with this gift. Responsibility. His talks with his mother developed the strong sense of self and values that have allowed him to achieve his dream and make him so likeable.

Brad's sensitivity to the world around him has been a greater gift than his good looks. And his sensitivity has brought both joy and pain. Brad recalled, "Growing up, I was an insider—inside everything, like the cool stuff at school—but always looking out. Because it wasn't quite enough or something. Insider looking out—that's perfect. That sums it all up." And, remarkably, *insider-looking-out* does depict a side of Brad. Even then, the *looking-out* part of Brad was restless with an ambition he couldn't yet name, a knowledge that Missouri was tiny compared to the world and an inkling that religion didn't fit with how he saw life turning out.

He once told journalist Chris Heath, "You're talking to a guy who's always had this congenital sadness. I don't know where it comes from. I don't know what it is…the state of the world, the state of yourself. I don't know. I had a very easy childhood, deprived of nothing per se, you know…I mean, turn on the news. I just always had so many questions growing up—why this, why the state of the world, why does God want this? Congenital sadness. It always comes up, for no reason. I don't know what it is." Most probably, Brad suffers from a mild depression, a state in which many artists find themselves. It is normal for people who are sensitive, empathetic and intelligent like Brad. Surprisingly, Brad, despite this congenital sadness, was also an insider.

But then, if Brad commits to something, he throws himself, whatever the risks, into it 100 percent. And Brad was committed to being a popular all-around-great-high-school guy. He participated in everything. In sports, he played tennis, baseball, football and basketball for the Kickapoo High School Chiefs. Brad was also involved in choir, drama, student government and the debate team. He even joined the forensic club, and most important, he earned good grades all around. Not that Brad was only a straight-ahead guy; he was mischievous, which led to some bad behavior. When a journalist asked, "Were you a good student? A troublemaker?" Brad replied, "Both. You know, on the class cabinet, but getting suspended." In his senior year, Brad had the honor of being voted Best Dressed by his class. As he is now, Brad was driven to succeed, but then he was driven to please others more so than himself. Perhaps this drive was his way of being responsible for and balancing the blessing of his good looks.

Sometime in early elementary school, Brad discovered girls, as legend goes, when he and some chums found a stack of *Playboy* magazines at a construction site. As for the pictures, Brad said, "Well, I was very impressed. I was just so overwhelmed." From all accounts, he has been girl-crazy ever since. There was a period in seventh grade when Brad's basement was the venue for make-out sessions. Brad found his good looks and charm useful when it came to getting girls to attend these soirees. "The girls overdid it with that flavored lip gloss," Brad remembered, "But we didn't know it at the time—we thought it was fine." His mother didn't think it was

> ...Brad was driven to succeed, but then he was driven to please others more so than himself.

15

fine, and she kept a not-so-subtle eye on the situation. "My mom always made a lot of noise before opening the door to the basement. She'd call down, 'Brad? Can I come down and get something out of the freezer?' Of course, you had to wonder why Mom needed a frozen steak at 10:00 at night."

But his early make-out sessions didn't mean that Brad grew up to be a womanizer or even promiscuous. He was simply practicing being the romantic he would become. He had his first girlfriend at the tender age of 14. Then came his serious teenage sweetheart, Sarah Vale, followed by other shorter-lived relationships, including one with Liza Stanzer who eventually decided she preferred Brad's brother, Doug, causing a short-lived falling-out between the brothers. She knew what she was doing though; she and Doug later married, and Brad became a proud uncle to their children.

More than girls, Brad loved movies. As a child, he found that they had a profound effect on him. He said once, "That was my experience as a child. That's why I love movies. Because someone demonstrated or articulated something that I had felt but never been able to put it that way, and it made sense to me. And someone showed me some clarity and it really moved me." Here, Brad revealed his artist's soul: the ability to place himself in an unknown situation and relate it to his own experience and feelings. Movies gave Brad a window into a world that made sense to him. While school bored him, movies engaged him and sparked his curiosity. He clearly remembers his experience of watching movies, at the local drive-in.

Brad counts *Saturday Night Fever* as a favorite: "…not because of the dancing, or the clothes but seeing these other cultures and these guys with their accents and the way they handled themselves and

> Movies gave Brad a window into a world that made sense to him. While school bored him, movies engaged him and sparked his curiosity.

talked. It blew my mind, and it got me on this quest for travel and other cultures." And *Butch Cassidy and the Sundance Kid:* "I remember seeing *Butch Cassidy* at a drive-in. I cried in the end, when they died. I just remember that so vividly. I was really embarrassed, and I didn't want my parents to see me crying, so I ducked down in the back seat and pretended I was asleep."

But truly, **Planet of the Apes** was the most memorable, and Brad asserts it was "the most brilliant film on religion ever made." The first time he watched it was at the drive-in—sitting on the hood of the car, drinking Kool-Aid and munching popcorn. Later there was a Planet of the Apes-a-thon, all five movies back to back, that Brad went to, alone except for the lunch his mom had made for him. "I think it's very accurate to religion in general today—don't shake the herd."

"Shaking the herd" was what Brad had to do in order to get to Hollywood. He started doing that when he finished high school and left for college.

chapter 2

Brother Pitt Goes to College

I had a great time in college. I learned more about being on my own than anything in a book. It's just as important to find out what you don't want to do as what you do want to do.

Going to college was never a question for Brad. With his academic achievement in high school and his sense of duty to his parents, Brad didn't consider other choices in how his life was to unfold. His ambition, at that point, was "to go to college, get a gal, get a house with a white picket fence…" And so, in 1982, like many young middle-class Americans, he started on this rite of passage: to spend the next four years immersed in college life. In a beat-up Buick Centurion

455, that his father gave him, Brad drove the 163 miles from Springfield to Columbia.

Although little has been written about Brad's college years, they are significant in many ways to his personal development and his later success. College gave Brad a wider window on the world than Springfield, distance from his family to find his distinct views and identity and a safe environment in which to explore a wilder and excessive lifestyle. These four years allowed a dutiful son from Missouri to break the chains of geography, religion and family in order to discover who he was and what he wanted.

To begin to understand Brad, it is important to understand his intelligence, his curiosity and his love of learning. A common problem that has plagued him throughout his career is the misconception that Brad is not very bright or—to be blunt—stupid. Nothing could be further than the truth. Very probably,

Although Brad is charming, it's not easy for him to talk about personal matters.

the notion comes from the characters he has played, along with Brad's public presentation, which is humble and honest. As Brad points out, he doesn't "have the East Coast vocabulary in which all I say is packaging. The upper East Coast schooling. It's very different from the private schooling in Missouri, you know, but I work on it."

It was a shock to him to learn that his manner would be perceived as a lack of intelligence: "Aidan Quinn said to me during *Legends*—and this was the first time I heard the phrase—'you're dumbing yourself down.' He [Quinn] said, 'You do this at times.' I had no idea. I was surprised. I think it was something I learned growing up—there's a big sense of that in a country mentality, in not wanting people to feel bad."

People who know Brad are quick to deny any question about his intelligence. Co-stars, directors, producers and friends note Brad can appear naive because Brad is naturally open and courteous. "It's true that Brad is very sweet, but people shouldn't be misled," Aidan Quinn said, "This is a warrior you're dealing with. He'll sometimes play a dumb country boy, but he's one of the most well-read actors I've worked with."

It's his nature. As Edward Norton, Brad's co-star in *Fight Club*, said, "I think it's a shame if politeness and humility are perceived as a kind of rube-ish disingenuousness."

When he is interviewed, he is very much himself; he doesn't promote himself as a neat little package the press can then present to the public. Although Brad is charming, it's not easy for him to talk about personal matters. Journalists, frustrated with his lack of communication, often walk away from an interview thinking,

"What a knucklehead!" "Well, he's a knucklehead, but he's very smart," said his good friend Catherine Keener. "Brad never tries to make people understand that he's smart."

In high school, Brad had shown talent in the sciences and the arts, and like his mother, he had the eye of a visual artist, so he had options when selecting his career. The Missouri School of Journalism has the distinction of being not only the world's first school of journalism but also one of the best. There, Brad entered the prestigious advertising program.

The school demands that their students have a broad liberal education on which to build their journalistic skills. So, over the four years Brad spent there, he took many arts and science courses in addition to learning the practice and theory of advertising. Near the end of his degree, he was considering a career as an advertising art director and was at the point where he was designing and presenting complete campaigns. However, Brad became increasingly frustrated when his professors rejected his work as being too "outside the box." "They were doggin' my ideas. They wanted the straight thing, and it was really boring." Little by little, he realized that he would be unhappy, and perhaps, even fail in his chosen career.

Religion continues to be an ongoing theme for Brad; several movies he has worked on have examined religion...

The 163 miles from home was enough distance for Brad to finally resolve the part of his childhood that haunted him—that what he saw happening in the world around him was not reflected in the Baptist faith in which he was raised. He left the Baptist church. "I remember one of the most pivotal moments I've had was when I finally couldn't buy the religion I grew up with. That was a big deal. It was a relief in a way that I didn't have to believe that anymore, but then I felt alone. It was this thing I was dependent on."

Although Brad found it oppressive to be raised with someone else's views, he admires his parents' dedication. Talking to his mom about his loss of faith was heartbreaking, but Brad later said that they had spent many hours discussing it. Several months after Brad left the Church, his family left the Baptist religion for a non-denominational one. Brad didn't follow; he was done with religion. "I think once you give up religion, you've got to give up all religions. That's the way it seems to me. Everyone has his own religious code, and that's what I respect. It's a beautiful thing. Actually, it's huge. But I just couldn't keep it from what I saw along the road."

Religion continues to be an ongoing theme for Brad; several movies he has worked on have examined religion, such as *The Devil's Own*, which explores the Irish conflict between Catholics and Protestants. Around the time that movie was made, Brad said, "Religion is at best a pacifier and at worst, barbaric. People who live in a vacuum get very scared of people living in a different way. What threat is it to you if a gay man is kissing another gay man on the street? He's not coming into your home. This is public territory. Why does it f*** you up?"

PITT FAN FACT

Girls who attended college with Brad were treated to a calendar featuring a pin-up picture of him. They were also treated to a strip show (though not the full Monty) that Brad performed for charity.

His education also introduced him to an interest that, as he matures, is growing stronger all the time. In fact, it may become a greater fascination to Brad than making films—modern architecture. He discovered his interest in it while taking an elective course needed for his degree. One of his buddies was taking the course, and it was supposed to be easy. It "blew his mind" that houses could be something other than traditional. Even after discovering his immediate love for the world of architecture, Brad decided not to study it during his college days. "School was about getting out of classes instead of learning. And the architectural school was tough! They were studying day and night! I mean, I was in college, man!"

And college was a place and time where Brad got to play, and play hard. Once there, he moved into a frat house, after joining the Sigma Chi fraternity. According to its website, Sigma Chi fraternity's purpose "is to cultivate an appreciation of and commitment to the ideals of friendship, justice and learning." According to Brad, the fraternity was more interested in promoting an *Animal House* lifestyle than such ideals. In fact, his old chapter was suspended in 2002 for repeated violations of the fraternity's policy on drugs and alcohol.

About his residence Brad recalls, "It was incredible just to get away from home living with a bunch of guys. That school kind of revolves around a keg. We had this idea of *Animal House*, and there was definitely that aspect. Without a doubt, it was a highlight.

Then, like everything, you grow out of it." Getting that kind of lifestyle out of his system in college served him well when he got to Hollywood and would have to learn to deal with fame and everything that goes along with it, including the party aspect. For some young actors, such as River Phoenix, with whom Brad was slated to work in *Interview with a Vampire*, the results can be deadly.

> It took four years at college for Brad to identify what he wanted to do with his life. "You keep finding things in little increments. Each of these increments led me to say, 'You know what? I don't want to do this.'" His classmates were getting married or applying for jobs, and he didn't want to do either. Brad needed an escape from the conservative middle-class life everyone he knew was about to enter.

Like many people who grow up loving movies, Brad had a secret desire to be an actor. And like most people, he had never thought about it seriously, other than fleeting thoughts of "I could do that" when watching some guy who was his age perform in movies. Brad had let the geographical distance of Hollywood hold him back from pursuing his dream, but in the last month before graduation, he felt he had nothing to lose. His father's words, spoken a decade earlier must have come back to him: "Don't do it unless you love it." As Brad put it, "I had always wanted to be in the movies. I was in my fourth year of college and a week before graduation, and I thought if only I went

Although Brad did not graduate, his education was not wasted. It taught Brad valuable skills such as discipline, memorization and the tools with which to analyze scripts...

to California, maybe I could get a shot. I felt I had to get over there. I was majoring in a subject I didn't like and knew I wasn't cut out for. So I did not hand in my paper, did not graduate, scraped every bit of money I had and just left."

Although Brad did not graduate, his education was not wasted. It taught Brad valuable skills such as discipline, memorization and the tools with which to analyze scripts—useful skills for an actor. And besides acting, Brad benefited from gaining greater world knowledge—something to appease the *looking out* part of him.

What clinched it for Brad was finding a place to crash. A friend, whose father had a place in Los Angeles, told him he could stay there. Although Brad knew nothing about how movies were made, he was confident that his charm and good looks would be enough to get him through the door. Besides, if acting didn't pan out, he could pursue a career in art direction.

> Brad didn't tell his parents about leaving school. He knew in his heart and in his head that he was done, but he was concerned that his parents, having paid for his education, wouldn't "understand that what I got out of college was very valuable, even if I didn't have a piece of paper to prove it." He also lied about what he was doing in California. He told them he was attending the prestigious Art Center College of Design in Pasadena.

Later on, Brad realized that the reason he was able to make such a crazy decision was because of his supportive parents: "I could do that because I had a base. In the back of my head, I knew I had a family I could fall back on. My folks had always said,

'Do what you gotta do. We'll be here when you get back.' It wasn't until I got older that I realized I was blessed with these feelings."

At the time, Brad felt, "It was such a relief. I was coming to the end of college, and the end of my degree and the beginning of my chosen occupation." And so, following his dream, a choice now etched into Hollywood legend, with $325 in his pocket, Brad took off in his Nissan named Runaround Sue to chase his dream.

chapter 3

go west,
Young Man

It's up to you. If you've got anything more in you, it's up to you to show it.

In May of 1986, 22-year-old Brad Pitt drove the I40 to reach his destined home. But it wasn't until the summer of 1991 that he ascended to stardom. When he reached L.A., Brad had five years of struggle ahead of him. Talking to journalists about his efforts isn't something Brad is fond of. Many Hollywood stars have the same story—it's called "making it." Brad reflected, "What's interesting to me now is that a kid who had never been farther west than Wichita, Kansas, loaded up his car until he couldn't even see behind him and drove to that crazy city. I remember going to the Grand Canyon. I was thrilled by the whole journey. Then I got to L.A., and there was so much smog, and I realized that I didn't know anyone. And I was like, 'God, this is kinda depressing.'

So I got a Quarter Pounder with cheese and a large fries. And I got the newspaper and looked for work as an extra. The first couple nights, I had to crash in the car."

Brad knew nothing about the business or the craft of acting, but he knew enough to expect hardship. He'd given himself a year and if, by the end of that year, he wasn't earning money, then he'd pack away his acting dreams and move on. And so he slogged, with a laid-back, go-with-the-flow attitude that soon would be considered typical of Brad. For the first year and half, Brad slept on the floor. He stayed at the house of his college friend's father for a month, before shacking up with a bunch of guys who were pursuing the same dream: "There were eight guys in one room, no furniture, each with our own pile of clothes stacked up and a separate sheet for all of us on the floor."

Like many high-ranking stars, Brad held the required series of weird and demeaning jobs. But that's the game he had to play—finding work that kept him fed and housed, but that was flexible enough that he could go to an audition on short notice. "There was a place called the Job Factory, and every week they list all of these odd jobs. Those jobs kept me in Captain Crunch and peanut butter and jelly. It finally got so bad that a buddy and I said, 'Let's see who can get the most humiliating job.' I won. I got a job with a restaurant called El Pollo Loco. I dressed up as a chicken, stood out on the corner of Sunset in 100° weather and flapped my wings for the grand opening. They liked me so much, they asked me back."

> It was one of Brad's more discouraging jobs that put him on the path that eventually led to his stardom. For a few months, Brad drove strippers around to private parties, sometimes three a night; he drove, played the music, collected the fee and got the girls back into the car. Despite not being the type of girls a guy would take home to meet his mom, Brad felt sorry for them. Like him, they were often from small towns, trying to make it in a big city.

It turned out that one of the dancers Brad had chauffeured had an actor friend who studied with Roy London, the legendary acting coach. London had helped many actors succeed, such as Jeff Goldblum, Michelle Pfeiffer and Geena Davis. Brad joined one of his classes, and the six years he spent under Roy's tutelage is the sum of the training he has as an actor. Roy London was quick to recognize Brad's potential. His good looks were impressive, but could only take Brad so far. By training him in the basics of the dramatic method, London worked with Brad, developing his technique and honing his craft. London introduced Brad not only to artistic side of acting, but also to the business side, the side that gets an actor work. Soon, Brad was looking for an agent and attending open casting calls.

Again, fate stepped in. One of his classmates needed a male partner to read a scene with her for an audition for an agent. She asked Brad. As legend has it, Brad showed up, unwashed and relaxed—because he wasn't the one auditioning, he didn't make much of an effort. His relaxed attitude allowed his natural talent to shine, and it was he, not his classmate, who ended up with the key to an actor's success: an agent.

With an agent backing him, Brad began to get auditions more often, and soon, with more success. His first few appearances on film were as an extra in films such as *Less Than Zero* and *No Man's Land*. In *Less Than Zero*, Brad's job was to stand in a doorway during a party scene. He was paid only $38, but he was excited about working as an extra on a movie set. Of course, at that time, he had no idea how big a star he'd eventually become.

Roy London and his agent felt Brad's career would be best served starting in television, where he could get acting experience, begin building his resume and determine whether he could deal with the ugly, back-stabbing underworld of Hollywood. He landed his first role in the nighttime soap *Dallas*: "I was in three episodes, probably for about a total of four minutes. I was some reject boyfriend, an idiot. I just had to sit there on the couch and smile and s***." It wasn't a juicy role, but it did get Brad noticed.

Dallas was enough to get him some buzz, including an interview with *Tiger Beat*. In it, 22-year-old Brad shed some insight into his experiences: "Since I have come out here, I have really been

One story in particular captures his need to find love during this period.

a loner, investing all my money and time [into] making it. It's so important to me. I really don't go out that much—just with my buddies, and we'll go catch a flick. I can have just as much fun by myself. I read, write, listen to tunes." The solitude Brad talks about here is striking, considering his popularity in school and college. The lean years gave Brad focus, and the time he needed to sort through his values and build a strong and independent identity.

His solitude was briefly interrupted when he began dating his *Dallas* on-screen girlfriend, Shalane McCall. Although his relationship with McCall was short-lived—a reported six weeks—it shows the pattern Brad fell into: falling in love with his co-stars. And, desperate for a girlfriend, Brad was a young man looking to fall in love, which reportedly he did easily and often.

One story in particular captures his need to find love during this period. His girlfriend, Jill Schoelen, whom he was to meet on the set of his first film, was filming a cheesy remake of *Phantom of the Opera* in Hungary. Jill wasn't having a good time. She would call Brad in tears, telling him she was lonely and having problems during filming. One night, she was more upset than usual and Brad, spending $600 of the $800 he had, flew overnight via London and headed straight to the set. Jill broke up with him at dinner, telling him she had fallen in love with the director. Brad left immediately. He didn't even spend the night in Hungary.

After *Dallas*, Brad steadily won small roles in several popular TV series, including *Another World*, *21 Jump Street* (a teen-cop drama starring Johnny Depp), *Head of the Class* (where he met and then briefly dated Robin Givens), *Freddy's Nightmares*, *Growing Pains* and *thirtysomething* (created by Edward Zwick who later directed Brad in *Legends of the Fall*). Although these roles had nothing to do with why he wanted to do movies, he was proud. "I was thinking, 'This is so great!' I come from the Ozark Mountains. We don't have that kind of stuff where I grew up. I move out there and all of a sudden, I'm in the middle of it. Fantastic!" Even better, he was earning a living in the industry. He finally called his parents and let them know what he was really doing in California. "I kinda thought it was something like that," his father replied to Brad's news.

With each role, Brad was gaining confidence that he had more to offer than his good looks. From the responses he was getting, he became more assured; he had natural talent—a talent that was slowly developing. Brad's confidence allowed him to stand up to his mentors, London and his agent, who were pushing to get him into sitcoms. It wasn't that sitcoms didn't appeal to Brad (he was a huge fan of *Friends* long before he met Jennifer Aniston), but he sensed the work wouldn't play to his strengths. Brad was beginning to understand the business: "You get pushed in this business. You just gotta push back harder. Because it comes down to you."

Even though he was successful in determining his direction, his first feature-length work was not for film, but a well-made TV movie called *A Stoning in Fulham County*. The movie tells the story of an Amish family, whose youngest member—a baby—is stoned to death in one of many incidents of religious harassment the family had suffered. Brad had a small role as the remorseful Teddy Johnson, one of the youths involved in the stoning. Intelligent and provocative, the movie was a quality credit on Brad's resume.

While **Cutting Class** has little entertainment value, Brad came across well as the film's all-American high school athlete, complete with sporty red convertible and cheerleader girlfriend.

This was not the case with the movie that followed. Brad's first sizeable role on the silver screen was in *Cutting Class*, a cheap spoof on slasher horror movies popular at the time, like the *Friday the 13th* series. The horror genre has traditionally

Glory Days, TV (1990)

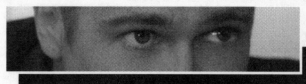

been a starting ground for many emerging stars, screenwriters and directors, and Brad was no different. At the time, Brad was pleased to receive third billing; later, however, he removed the credit from his resume. While *Cutting Class* has little entertainment value, Brad came across well as the film's all-American high school athlete, complete with sporty red convertible and cheerleader girlfriend. The actress who played his girlfriend? Jill Schoelen.

Brad's next role was smaller and in a film not much better than *Cutting Class*. Released in 1989, *Happy Together* was, as Leonard Maltin described it, "a slight, predictable romantic comedy." Brad neither minded the small role nor the lackluster reception—it increased his visibility. Brad was learning that progress in the movie business came from becoming a familiar face to casting directors.

Brad's next offer caused a problem. He was approached to do a commercial advertising Levi's jeans in Europe. Doing the ad, Brad feared, might compromise his wish to be taken seriously as an actor. He was aware of the effect of his looks; since childhood, he had known that he could coast through life on his good looks. But to do so would go against his sense of ethics. Whatever he accomplished in life, he wanted to achieve it through his abilities, rather than his physical beauty. After some deliberation, he decided to do the ad because of the easy cash and the European exposure. Exposure, indeed! The sexy ad featured Brad stripping off his jeans and using them to climb out of a jail cell. In Europe, he became an instant sex symbol.

Back in the States, Brad was through with television work; television, however, was not through with Brad. In fact, the next three out of four projects Brad did were for TV, and each took him closer to his breakthrough role. The first was a lead in a new series created by the then one-year-old Fox TV network. The series, *Glory Days*, was a comedy-drama, which followed the lives of four friends, newly graduated from high school. As usual, his character, Walter Lovejoy, was significantly younger than Brad's 26 years. Sadly, the series, although well reviewed, fell victim to Fox's policy of canceling shows after six episodes if their ratings didn't soar. Brad, hoping to use the series as

Across the Tracks (1991)

a transition into film as Johnny Depp had done with *21 Jump Street*, was disappointed.

His next role was in the TV movie, *The Image*, starring the immensely talented British actor, Albert Finney. Although his character had about 10 minutes of screen time, that time was exclusively with Finney.

> **Brad followed his solid performance on the small screen with another high school athlete role on the big screen. *Across the Tracks* was never destined to be a blockbuster, but it was a decent and convincing movie about two brothers competing for an athletic scholarship. The star was Ricky Schroeder, but Brad played the main character, the younger brother. In terms of acting, the role was hardly a stretch for Brad, but in terms of the business, the role was proof that Brad had what it took to carry a film.**

In his last role before landing *Thelma and Louise*, Brad returned to TV to star in the issue driven movie-of-the-week type drama, *Too Young Too Die?* The script was based on the true story of Amanda Sue Bradley, a sexually abused runaway who was the first minor to receive the death sentence. Its controversial story, one that was sure to stir up interest, attracted Brad. Besides, for the first time in his career, Brad got to play something other that the all-American high school athlete. He played the abusive druggie boyfriend, who convinces his girlfriend to commit murder. Taking the role in *Too Young to Die?* was a smart move. Brad received positive notices for the role, the best he'd had in his career. The actress who played his girlfriend? Juliette Lewis, Brad's first mature love and the woman he adored for the next three years.

Brad said, "My agents had been pushing me towards sitcoms. I knew that I had to find something ugly and real so I could prove to them that they were pushing me wrong. Then *Too Young to Die?* came along. I knew I was going to get the part. And I knew I was going to be very good friends with whoever played the young girl. It was just a feeling I had. Sometimes you get those little whispers in the ear."

For a man who had no place for religion in his heart, Brad had a lot of faith, and it got him through these lean years. And he was right: his five years of suffering for his art was about to end.

chapter 4

Taking Off

I knew that part [JD in Thelma and Louise] was going to come along. I can't explain it, but I knew it. Sometimes I was patient, sometimes I was anxious, but I knew. And then, when it did come along, I knew I was going to get it. I read it, and immediately I knew. I knew this guy to the end.

Outside of filming *Too Young to Die?* Brad and Juliette spent time together researching the technique of shooting up drugs. They watched films such as *Panic in Needle Park.* But it wasn't until the filming was finished that Brad realized he had romantic feelings for Juliette. The subject matter of the film had hardly been conducive, as Brad said mischievously, "It

was quite romantic, shooting her full of drugs and stuff." There was also a matter of their age difference. At 16, Juliette was 10 years younger than Brad and had little experience as an adult.

Driving home together after the shoot, Juliette recalled their trip: "We didn't say much. We listened to music. After that drive, we both knew we liked each other. We didn't even kiss. I was expecting it, because you move so fast these days. But he didn't—he gave me a hug. I tortured my best friend, Trish, over this for the next three weeks."

Brad did a lot of thinking over those three weeks. Suddenly, after seeing the possibility of getting what he wanted—a serious girlfriend—had come about, Brad was hesitant. He was hesitant because of Juliette's age and their different backgrounds, and he was unsure about embarking on a serious romance at this make-it-or-break-it point of his career. But Brad recognized

> Because they shared the same goal, were on the same path, at the same juncture, Brad decided that he and Juliette could be together and further their careers.

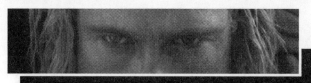

that Juliette was equally ambitious, and that she was at the same point in her career as he was in his. Juliette had also spent the last four years in what she called "sit-com hell." Neither of them wanted to go back there. Because they shared the same goal, were on the same path, at the same juncture, Brad decided that he and Juliette could be together and further their careers.

Unlike Brad's Baptist upbringing, Juliette's childhood was very free. But Juliette's parents gave the same thing to their daughter as Brad's parents gave him. Juliette said, "My parents raised me in a really unique way, they didn't fill me with self-doubt. There are a lot of people who don't want to think of their kids as having sex or really awful experiences. But the thing is, you have to experience these things sooner or later. My parents made me feel as though I was always worth something." This shared foundation of self-confidence and inner faith was a strong enough bond for them to begin a deep and lasting relationship. Brad and Juliette spent the next three years together, building their separate careers and seeing each other through their respective first encounters with fame: Brad in *Thelma and Louise* and Juliette in *Cape Fear*.

Brad's involvement with *Thelma and Louise*, or as he calls it, the "$6000 Orgasm," began as it would with any actor of Brad's caliber: a casting call. His agent set up an audition, but Brad wasn't hopeful because casting calls rarely end successfully. He was even less hopeful when he arrived for his audition. The casting director

Thelma and Louise (1991)

kindly let him know that director Ridley Scott had his heart set on William Baldwin playing the part of JD. Still, because he would actually be auditioning with Geena Davis, a big-time Hollywood actress, Brad went ahead. "It just sparked," Brad said of the audition, and so it was a bit of a disappointment when Scott went ahead and hired Baldwin. It was more than a pleasant surprise when Brad got the call later telling him he had the part. At the last minute, Baldwin had pulled out to take a bigger role in the firefighting film *Backdraft* directed by Ron Howard.

> **Thelma and Louise** was a departure for Scott, who had established his name as a director with such films as **Alien** and **Blade Runner**, and that is why Scott signed onto the project: "The main reason I chose to do this film was that I'd never done anything like it before. This is a film where the emphasis—the driving force, if you will—is almost character driven, rather than where a spaceship comes from."

Thelma and Louise was not only a departure for Scott, but also for the road movie genre, which had been the exclusive territory of male characters. Here, it's a story of two women. Thelma (Geena Davis) and Louise (Susan Sarandon) are best friends who are fed up with the piggish behavior of the men in their lives. To get some perspective, they plan a weekend getaway. A series of unfortunate events forces these ordinary women to become outlaws as they take an increasingly desperate road trip across the southern United States. Scott articulated the film's appeal: "Rarely do scripts come along that are about truth. This one most certainly is, and it never deviates from that. It's humorous, it's dramatic, it's even slightly mythical in proportions. That's just about everything you can ask from a really good story."

The women's encounter with JD is one of those unfortunate events. He's a cowboy hitchhiker who the duo picks up. His boyish southern charm wins over Thelma, and they end up in bed, where JD gives Thelma her first orgasm. He turns out to be a hustler, taking the all the money ($6700) the women have and pushing them into robbery as a means of survival.

Although Brad makes the role of JD look effortless, pulling off that kind of character is tricky. He has to be charming enough to make the audience understand why Thelma falls for him, but dangerous enough that the audience believes his actions. Besides his scenes with Thelma, the detective following the women later interrogates JD. Played by Gene Hackman, the detective reveals the spineless criminal that lies beneath JD's charms. For a character with 10 minutes of screen time, JD is complex, and Brad pulled it off beautifully. He said, "I loved that guy. He just had it all figured out. He knew what worked for him, and he was so damned nonchalant."

Thelma and Louise was a low-budget film, so it was surprising how well it did in the box office. By the end of the summer, it was competing nicely with the season's blockbusters. Based on its good reviews and word-of-mouth, the attendance grew. Of course, the fact that the film sparked huge controversy about the question of it being a fascist feminist movie with a male-bashing agenda didn't hurt.

> **The official premiere foreshadowed what would become common in Brad's life. Juliette recalled, "Everyone was screaming, 'Brad! Brad! Over here!' The flashbulbs are exploding in your face. It was like a brainwashing trip."**

Brad also knew he had to reinforce his new status as a film star. So, before *Thelma and Louise* was released to the public, Brad took advantage of the Hollywood buzz surrounding his performance—he was onto his next project, an ensemble piece called *The Favor*, in which he played Elliot Fowler. Luckily for Brad, the movie wasn't released to cinemas because the producers' studio, Orion, went bankrupt. Instead, it went straight to video in 1994. A romantic comedy about four friends, *The Favor* suffered from a weak story and an even weaker script. Although Brad held his own against veterans Bill Pullman and Elizabeth McGovern, the movie was a poor choice to follow his success in *Thelma and Louise*. The only interesting thing about this flick is that Brad wears glasses.

With fortune watching over him and sparing his career from the release of *The Favor*, Brad moved onto another film, an art-house film in which he played the title character, *Johnny Suede*. Throughout his career, Brad has consistently chosen projects that in some way reflect or, as Brad puts it, "answer to" his last project. *Johnny Suede* required different acting muscles and presented

> **"Another sex symbol. How boring. That's just what the world needs. Somebody who symbolizes sex."**

Johnny Suede (1991)

another side of Brad than did the roles of JD and Elliot Fowler. Whereas JD and Fowler used Brad's sex appeal, Johnny Suede was the opposite. And after the combination of the Levi's ad and *Thelma and Louise*, Brad was concerned that he would be trapped by his looks. He scorned, "Another sex symbol. How boring. That's just what the world needs. Somebody who symbolizes sex." But while Brad could deflect his sex symbol status with sarcasm, he still had the same fear he had suffered earlier in his career when his agents were shaping him into a teen idol.

The character of Johnny Suede is the opposite of a sex symbol—a lost soul stuck in his romanticism of the 1950s, a Ricky Nelson "wannabe" with big hair and an obsession with suede. Brad called him "anti-glamorous," and he delighted: "…just look at Johnny Suede's underwear. I ripped forever to get those things to look like that. I stretched for hours. I even wanted to put a skid mark in them, but they wouldn't let me."

The brainchild of the film's director, Tom DiCillo, *Johnny Suede* was created in DiCillo's theater school days. Later, DiCillo developed a one-man show as Johnny Suede and performed it in New York. DiCillo then left theater for film and drifted into becoming a cameraman. The job paid the bills, but it didn't feed his creative side. He went back to his one-man show and adapted it into a screenplay, which was accepted into the prestigious Sundance Institute for a workshop. Founded by Robert Redford to encourage indigenous and independent filmmaking, the Sundance Institute plays an incredibly important role in the industry. DiCillo is an example of the institute's importance. Because of his screenplay's connection with Sundance, he was able to find financing for the film and bring Brad on board.

> DiCillo had first wanted to perform the role but he decided, being a first-time director and screenwriter, it would serve the film better if he cast another actor in the role. Giving up the role was difficult, especially when actors began to audition for him. He felt the actors just didn't understand the character, but Brad was different. He says, "It wasn't until Brad came in and **damn,** there was just something very magical about it. He took off his boots and did this monologue about suede. I was immediately convinced that this was **the** guy. He wasn't afraid to show that Johnny is this guy with all these problems on his sleeve."

The film tells the whimsical and surreal story of Johnny Suede, a man who has no inner life because he's invested himself entirely in his outward appearance. He receives what he believes is a sign—a pair of black suede shoes fall from the sky and hit him on the head—that he is meant to be a 1950s rock idol. Trouble is, he's all-looks-and-no-talent and until he meets Yvonne, played by Catherine Keener, he lacks the self-awareness to understand. As Brad points out, "The end of the movie is really the beginning of Johnny. He wakes up one morning and realizes he's been an idiot. He didn't need the hair."

The filming of **Johnny Suede** did not go smoothly because of tension between the director and the star. Brad took the brunt of the blame, earning, unfairly, his first mark as a "difficult" actor. The situation itself should be blamed: a novice director who had created the character and who could not separate himself from his creation while directing a young, inexperienced actor who related to the character too deeply. Both men were too attached to the character and lacked the experience to understand and deal with that.

The tensions often found on movie sets are part of making movies. Actors and directors may have different ideas about characters, or they may have different processes that conflict with each other. Add to these conflicts the pressure caused by the incredible expense of making movies and tempers can flare. Brad has little formal training but a lot of natural talent. His process, then, is one of play and investigation. Instinctive actors, like Brad, require time and space to discover a moment, which can involve many takes. Other actors,

Brad now had three flops in a row. Nobody was counting, however, because his fame only increased.

Cool World (1992)

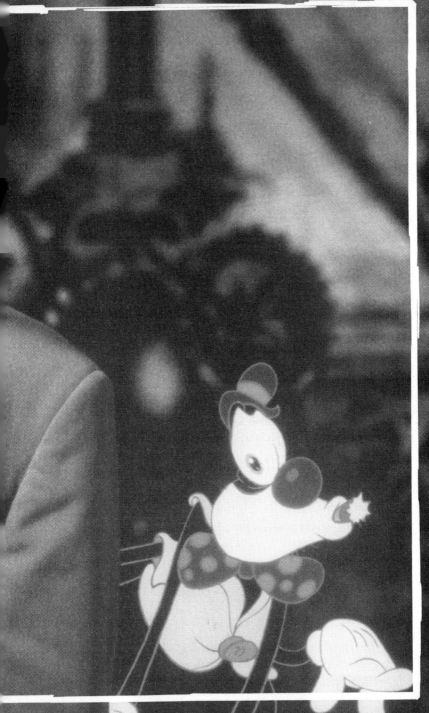

like Julia Roberts, are more cerebral. They know exactly what the moment is and can capture it in one or two takes. Both processes can make for incredible performances.

Brad's performance as Johnny Suede earned him good notices. In the *Village Voice* review, J. Hoberman wrote, "It is DeCillo's good fortune to have Brad Pitt play his sincerely self-absorbed hero. Indeed, for a stylish exercise in cool, *Johnny Suede* is extremely well acted. *Johnny Suede* may look like a cartoon, but it is deep enough to leave open questions...." For the art-house crowd, the movie was an instant cult classic. For the mainstream audience, *Johnny Suede* came and went unnoticed. However, Brad proved to himself and to casting agents that he could play roles other than the sex symbol.

Brad's next project didn't do well in the box office either. More, critics universally trashed the movie, and even Brad's performance didn't escape unscathed. *Cool World* was a blend of live action and animation that starred Brad as Detective Frank Harris; Gabriel Byrne, a well-respected Irish actor, as the cartoonist; and Kim Bassinger as a cartoon who becomes human. Inevitably, *Cool World* was compared to blockbuster *Who Framed Roger Rabbit?* It couldn't compete.

> Famed **Fritz the Cat** creator Ralph Bakshi directed the movie, meant it to be an adult-themed approach to animation. But from the outset, confusion ruled. Even Bakshi, the film's creator, was unable to pinpoint the tone: "It has horror moments, it has **film noir** detective pulp moments, and it has pure cartoon moments."

Never having worked with live actors before, Bakshi left them to their own devices. But as the actors were doing their scenes against a blue screen without their animated scene partners, they needed an experienced director to help bring out their characters. As a result, in the film, the animation dominates, and the human element is lost.

> Whether **Cool World** is considered a brave, but failed, experiment or a box office disaster, the result is the same: it was a flop.

Brad now had three flops in a row. Nobody was counting, however, because his fame only increased. In 1992, after the release of *Cool World*, Brad had a moment to reflect: "This place has been good to me, but everyone makes judgments about it from afar. There are people, including me, who thought happiness was the place. This is why I left Missouri. I've found that happiness is a way of travel." Happiness, like religion, is a recurring theme for Brad, and tracing his views on happiness shows us the map of a man maturing. The recognition that happiness is in the process and not the product was Brad's first stop.

chapter 5

learning to fly

You can't just cash in. It seems to me that if you take a role, you take it because there's something you kinda want to check out. You know? In your own mind.

In 1992, *A River Runs Through It* was released. It would be the first of several epic productions that made good use of both Brad's looks and his talent. Based on Norman MacLean's autobiographical novella of the same name, the story resonated with Brad. "Here's a kid who grew up in a religion, who grew up with someone else's views. But then he starts to find contradictions, and he eventually self-destructs. *River* just makes me so sad. The guy needed so badly for his family—for his older brother—to understand him, and they never could."

A River Runs Through It was directed by Robert Redford,

and like all of his directing projects, it was his baby. He was deeply moved after reading the story about a father and his two sons, who are able to communicate only through a shared passion for fly-fishing. It took Redford five years to convince MacLean to release the cinematic rights to him. Always a perfectionist, Redford was even more driven to do justice to the author's material when, four months into production, MacLean died.

In keeping with his artistic vision, Redford spent time assembling a cast that he felt would best tell the story. First cast was Craig Sheffer as the older brother, the character who tells us the story and through whose eyes we see the story unfold. As the father, Redford cast Tom Skerrit. But casting the younger brother Paul was more difficult, because that character had to possess an aura of golden promise as well as self-doom within his personality.

Redford auditioned many young actors. As River Phoenix, a contender for the role, astutely commented, "I auditioned—me and a thousand other guys. I had a good meeting with Redford, but I think he's gonna find the guy—the guy who is just that image—the Montana mountain boy, fly-fisherman image…" Phoenix, with his well-publicized strange upbringing, couldn't fit this image, but Brad, Missouri mountain boy, could. He too had auditioned for the role, but his audition, as Brad described it, was "s***."

A River Runs Through It (1992)

Not willing to let a bad audition lose him a part that resonated with him so deeply and would take his career to another level, Brad found another way to keep himself in the running. He and pal Dermot Mulroney videotaped a few scenes from the movie and sent them to Redford. What he didn't know was that Redford was already interested in Brad and had asked around to see if the young actor was good to work with. The answer was a definite Yes! Redford told reporters he cast Brad for his "golden-boy" image, which fit Redford's idea of the character. "There's no sign of trouble in his face," said Redford.

Problems with adapting a literary work for cinema made filming difficult. While a book can delve into the depths of a character's thoughts, film is visual and the inner workings of a character's mind must be revealed either through dialogue or through action. Redford admitted later, "I thought this was a book that would be almost impossible to do. It has two elements—it is very literary and very lyrical. Film is not a literary medium, obviously, and in America at least, such things don't go down very well. Lyricism in film is treated with a great deal of cynicism. There were two hurdles right there."

A River Runs Through It is a testament to Redford as a director, because he managed to overcome those hurdles, and as a result, the movie did much better than anticipated at the box office. As well, the film received an Oscar for its cinematography and an Oscar nomination for its adapted screenplay. Redford was also nominated for a Golden Globe as the film's director. The reviews were good, and many reviewers singled out Pitt for particular praise, while others seemed to focus on the remarkable physical similarity between Pitt and Redford as a younger man. *Village Voice* went as far as to condemn Redford, calling his casting choice "some narcissistic impulse." In any case, the film marked Brad's ascent to a higher quality of film.

"Well, of my part, there could have been a little more back story, maybe. But there's no getting around it. Redford did a fantastic job crafting that film, shaping it into chiseled granite."

While Brad is proud of the film, he thought his performance was weak and found it strange that it would receive more attention than his other performances. During filming, Brad was frustrated that he hadn't been allowed to develop his character fully, but he was aware that, as an actor, his needs were secondary to the needs of the film. Redford cast him for his golden-boy looks and paid more attention to how Brad was lit that his acting. As Brad said, "Well, of my part, there could have been a little more back story, maybe. But there's no getting around it. Redford did a fantastic job crafting that film, shaping it into chiseled granite. A film adapted from a book's got to take its own form—Redford did that."

> **The frustration that arose from conforming to Redford's vision and not exploring Paul's dark side influenced his next choice of role: the psychotic, serial killer Early Grayce in *Kalifornia*.**

The film tells the story of a journalist, played by David Duchovny, whose fascination with serial killers leads him to plan a road trip, choosing places to visit because of their serial killer connection. He plans to turn the journey into a book. His girlfriend, played by Michelle Forbes, is a professional photographer, and she comes along to take pictures. They advertise to find people to share the costs and adventure. Early and his girlfriend, played by Juliette Lewis, answer the ad. Once on the trip, the couple discovers that Early himself is a serial killer.

In an interview with *Sky Magazine,* Brad was asked if his attraction to playing Early was because the character was so gross. Brad responded affirmatively. "My character's a redneck. A real backwards hillbilly, you know. He's a guy with no morality. An idiot. He kills people as if they're bugs. He hasn't had many options so he's created his own ideas about right and wrong, and they're a bit off from what other people think. He creates things in his life for excitement, and one of them happens to be murder."

A River Runs Through It (1992)

The other attraction, of course, was working with Juliette again. The press had cast them as the Hollywood grunge couple, the "gorgeous grim twosome." Tabloids followed their fashion choices closely. Brad was delighted when the tabloids voted Juliette's cornrow hairdo as Worst Hair at the Oscars. He said, "I was so proud of her." The tabloids had also hinted at trouble between the couple, and it was true. Brad and Juliette's relationship was floundering: in their two and half years as a couple, they had actually spent very little time together. Brad had made five movies, all filmed on location: *Thelma and Louise* took him to Utah, *The Favor* to Oregon, *Johnny Suede* to New York, *Cool World* to Nevada and *A River Runs Through It* to Montana. Juliette had made four movies, *Crooked Heart*, filmed in Canada, *Cape Fear* in Florida, *Husbands and Wives* in New York and *That Night* in Pennsylvania. As Juliette said, "What's not easy is the separation. The problems aren't, 'Oh, you're making movies with other people, and you're gonna sleep with them.' He's the most naturally monogamous creature I've ever run into, male or female. The hard thing is keeping good communication when you're 3000 miles apart."

Geographical distance wasn't the only factor. While he was away, Brad continued, as always, on his journey of self-discovery. He discovered an easiness with drifting, being alone, letting himself wander and following his curiosity. He has often called himself a loner. He began his now-established practice of buying a bicycle at the beginning of each shoot and leaving it behind at the end. His bicycles gave him access to quick and easy transportation. They symbolized the freedom Brad needed, the freedom to follow his own path. In some ways, he was still breaking loose from his Baptist upbringing and the

As he said, "I wasn't under any pressure at all. You've got to see what's going on if your love's into it, because you've got to respect your love."

Kalifornia (1993)

middle-class values with which he was raised. He wasn't ready to surrender the self-determination of his path.

But, as press cuttings show at this time, Brad and Juliette had different ideas about their relationship. Juliette told *People* they were thinking of marriage, whereas Brad told *Cleo Magazine*, he wasn't ready to live with her: "I don't feel like we deserve to live together just yet. Not that anything's wrong, it's just that there's time for that, that's all I'm saying." Their different understandings about their relationship reflected a deeper divide—different life philosophies.

The largest philosophical division was Juliette's faith. In the 1980s, she and her father had become affiliated with the Church of Scientology, and during her relationship with Brad, Juliette strengthened her commitment to being a Scientologist. Founded in the 1950s by science-fiction writer L. Ron Hubbard, Scientology is part science fiction, part cult and part religion. Believing celebrities would be the best way of spreading his message, Hubbard targeted Hollywood specifically. Many movie stars, including John Travolta and Tom Cruise, have joined the Church.

Brad did not convert, but he attended several of the Church's classes. As he said, "I wasn't under any pressure at all. You've got to see what's going on if your love's into it, because you've got to respect your love." And that's exactly what Brad tried—respect. "Whatever helps you sleep at night, whatever helps you get up in the morning," he said. "As much as

I don't want anyone telling me how to live my life, I can't tell anyone how to live theirs."

After a brief split before filming for *Kalifornia* began, Brad was committed to giving the relationship a shot. He and Juliette had gone from working separately to enjoying helping each other. He didn't see the work as the basis of their relationship. Work was fun, but it was also what drove them "crazy" at the same time.

> His agents had suggested that Brad turn down the role in **Kalifornia**, but he couldn't. Finally, Brad felt secure enough that he could choose a film, not based on how much he'd make or how it could advance his career, but based purely on his personal artistic standards. It was a choice that he has repeated throughout his career: balancing movies that he likes as an actor with movies that he knows will keep his career going.

The character of Early Grayce fascinated Brad. To Brad, movies explore the motives behind characters' actions and provide an understanding of why people behave the way they do. What could be more challenging for Brad than climbing into the skin of a serial killer? It was hard to find anything likeable, but Brad managed: "He's a killer, but, you know, you can hear about someone who does something really horrible, then you begin to understand a little bit about where they came from…. This guy, Early Grayce, would have loved something in the beginning and had been completely slammed down—where he gave up and had no feelings—so that killing someone meant no more than killing a bug. That's the way I saw him."

Kalifornia is an ensemble piece—the suspense and horror depended on the characters, not special effects. Although not a box office hit, reviews were positive and some were positively raves. Most were extremely taken with Brad and Juliette's performances. Respected *Rolling Stone Magazine* film critic Peter Travers wrote, "Don't look for logic—it's the quartet of actors that keeps you riveted. Pitt is outstanding, all boyish charm and then a snort that exudes pure menace. He and Lewis, once lovers off-screen, play this flapdoodle with enough urgency to make the suspension of disbelief worthwhile."

Undaunted by low box office numbers, Brad's work in **Kalifornia** was something he was proud of. For an actor who was his own worst critic, admitting pride in a performance means a lot. His mood was much lighter than it was after he'd finished **A River Runs Through It**. And as another actor treat, he took a cameo role in **True Romance**, an older script of Quentin Tarantino's, which was dusted off after Tarantino's success with **Reservoir Dogs**.

In it, Brad played the permanently stoned roommate of the best friend of the main character, played by Christian Slater. His part took only a few days to film, but Brad especially liked playing Floyd because "he gets everyone killed." Brad based his characterization on a friend who'd come to visit him in L.A. for a few days and stayed for a few months.

True Romance was a great success, which was hardly a surprise. The combination of director Tony Scott and writer

To Brad, movies explore the motives behind characters' actions and provide an understanding of why people behave the way they do.

True Romance (1993)

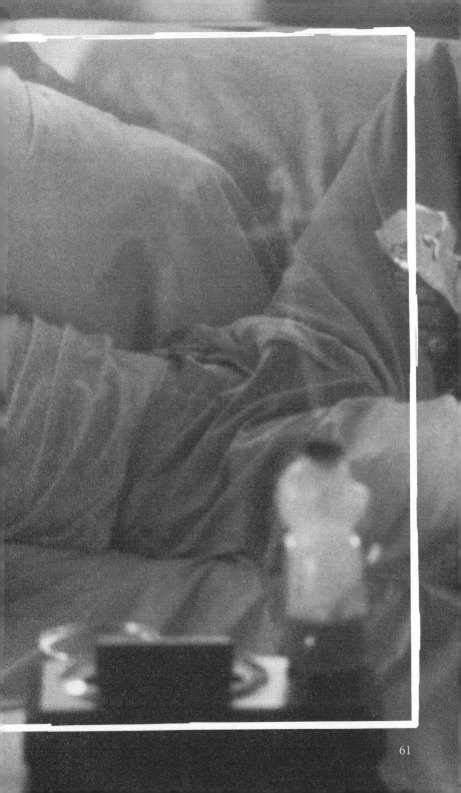

Quentin Tarantino, along with stars such as Gary Oldman, Dennis Hopper, Christopher Walken and Val Kilmer playing cameos, was unbeatable. What was surprising was how often Brad was singled out for praise amid all these giants.

True Romance wrapped in February 1993. In less than a year, Brad turned 30. He decided to break it off with Juliette instead of letting their on-and-off-again relationship continue to drift. Their differences were too deep to resolve, and Brad had grown tired of what he called the "Sid and Nancy" aspect the press had latched onto. While the actual details of their relationship and breakup were private, Brad and Juliette had clearly loved each other. He later said, "She had her own views. It was one of the greatest relationships I've ever been in. The problem is, we grow up with this vision that love conquers all, and that's just not so, is it?" The nature of romantic love became yet another theme Brad has continued to explore and develop as he matured.

Whereas his love for Juliette changed, his respect for her work did not. "I'd work with her again in a second. You could have some powerful stuff out there," he said. "I still love the woman. There's some real genius there. I had a great time with her."

Sadly, Juliette's genius, which was so present in the films *Cape Fear*, *Husbands and Wives* and *Natural Born Killers*, dimmed after their breakup. She became addicted to drugs and suffered a breakdown. Only recently does Juliette seem to be poised to let her genius take her to stardom.

Breaking up with Brad was the beginning of her downward slide. About the breakup, she said later, "It wasn't cut and dried. It wasn't totally breaking up, so I lost myself for a while. I felt bad about myself, and the thing about doing movies when your going through personal stuff is that you've got to feel good enough to be in front of a camera. It's a distant thing now, but a couple years ago, it was a huge change, and I had to remember that I had once lived alone and had my own pride and my own ideas. There was so much more to it than the relationship. It was also where I was in my life."

chapter 6

Of Legends and Vampires

Movies are very complicated. You don't realize what it takes to get a good movie. Sitting home in Missouri, I sure didn't.

Brad's next film had been in the works for 17 years. It was the baby of Edward Zwick, who had previously met Brad when Zwick was the creator of *thirtysomething*. His project was the cinematic adaptation of *Legend of the Falls*, a short story written by Jim Harrison and published in *Esquire* in 1978. At that time, Zwick, a 26-year-old film student, read the story and was immediately struck by the saga of the Ludlow family, a father

and his three sons growing up in Montana. To him, the cinematic qualities of such an epic account begged to be filmed. "I called the agents and publishers," Zwick recalled, "but I was still in school, and they laughed at me and told me the rights were owned by other people."

Zwick went on and built his career, first in TV and then in films, directing *About Last Night…*, *Leaving Normal* and *Glory*, before he was finally able to bring the period drama to the screen. *Legends* tells the tragic story of a father, Colonel Ludlow, who raises his three sons in the wilds of Montana after he leaves the cavalry to protest the treatment of Native Americans in the West. Inseparable while growing up, the three sons are torn apart by the trials of adulthood and the love of one woman, Susanna. Alfred, the eldest son, is dutiful and stoic. Samuel, the youngest, is idealistic and impulsive. Between them, both in age and in temperament is

He said, "I've always thought there would be someone better for most of the roles I've taken. But I knew I was the best one to play Tristan."

Legends of the Fall (1994)

Tristan, the central character, who has more in common with nature than with people. Beginning with the World War I, the story follows the three brothers as they try to find a place within the modern world.

> Since meeting Brad, Zwick had kept his eye on the rising star. He could see Brad as the complex Tristan, and so he sent a script to Brad two years before the project was slated for production. This was before even ***Thelma and Louise*** had been released. Of course, it was also before Zwick had convinced the studio to make the film.

Brad could relate to the brooding Tristan. He said, "I've always thought there would be someone better for most of the roles I've taken. But I knew I was the best one to play Tristan. I knew it the minute I read it. I knew the corners, I knew the bends in the road, knew exactly where it went. My difficulty was in trying to get others to see it the way I did. Films are very exhausting to make, so you'd better pick something that means something to you, and this one did." Describing the movie, Brad said, "It's big, it's bold, like a great big bottle of wine or something."

When Zwick got the project off the ground, Brad promised he would commit to playing Tristan. "One way we got this movie made was for me to defer a significant portion of my salary and for Brad to become my partner, doing that himself as well," recounted Zwick of his eventual success. However, the studio was hesitant about casting Brad, an unknown, as Tristan. But Zwick was firm that the role required "a force of nature," and Brad was the only actor able to embody that. After he signed Anthony Hopkins, the studio relaxed, and gave Zwick the go-ahead to cast Brad.

Hopkins was delighted to play Colonel Ludlow. During the filming, he told a reporter, "I turned up on the set the other day and said to the director, 'I've done Shakespeare, Ibsen and Chekhov, but I've been rehearsing to be a cowboy all my life.' Look at me—I'm not discovering a cure for cancer. I'm just getting paid to play out my childhood fantasies." Hopkins brought levity to the set, which was needed as shooting the film proved to be difficult.

To save money, the movie was shot in Canada, mostly on the Stoney First Nation Community, just outside Calgary, Alberta. The location was chosen because it is traditionally one of the driest places in Canada. However, in the summer of 1993, Calgary was hit with record-breaking amounts of rain. "For every beautiful cumulus cloud you see," said Zwick, "you don't see the three hours of us huddling under these awful tarps with lightning striking the dolly."

Legends of the Fall (1994)

Like fly-fishing for *A River Runs Through It*, Brad had to learn a new skill—horseback riding—and make it look like he'd been doing it all his life. Brad approached his challenge in his studied Zen-like way he had begun to adopt. Wanting to jump into the saddle like a real wrangler, Brad decided it was not a question of ability or experience, but one of physics. With the cameras rolling, he sprang into his saddle on the first take. "Listen, you just grab the pommel and kick," he explained. This seemingly glib explanation sheds light on Brad's success. He may not have religious faith, but he has faith that whatever life throws him, he'll land on his feet. His faith allows Brad to take risks, and taking risks is what good acting is about. Of course, there was one time that Brad fell off his horse, and the actor playing Alfred, Aidan Quinn, never let him forget it. He said, "I'm no horseman, but I never fell off my horse, like some people who will remain nameless."

For his three months of wet, grueling filming in Calgary, Brad rented a cabin, which became the place for cast and crew to hang out on Saturday nights. It was a great way to release tension. Aidan Quinn became a particularly good buddy. Their bond may have come from Brad's determination that Quinn be cast in the role. The role of Alfred, according to Brad, "could have easily gone wimpy. We needed somebody who'd be equal to Tristan, bringing nobility and strength to the role, and sexiness, of all things, and that's Aidan." Or else, their bond may have stemmed from their silly love of farts. One Saturday night, Quinn was given the name "Wind in his Pants."

Julia Ormond, who played Susannah, the woman who captures the hearts of all three brothers, shared Brad's cabin. She and Brad also became close. He marveled at her literariness, which he thought was classy. He said, "Julia brought a whole library of books. She read and wrote all the time." She was particularly important to Brad as support because, from the first week of shooting, the relationship between Brad and Zwick was difficult.

It's inevitable that tensions arise when two artists, equally passionate and committed, are involved in a creative process...

Brad's clashes with DiCillo during the filming of *Johnny Suede* were echoed in the filming of *Legends*. It's inevitable that tensions arise when two artists, equally passionate and committed, are involved in a creative process, the outcome of which is incredibly important to both. After several years of partnering to get the film to the point of production, Brad and Zwick shouldn't have been surprised that the process of bringing Tristan to life also brought clashes. By both men's accounts, they realized it was just part of getting the film done. And both men were faced with the added pressure of pushing Brad's scenes to the beginning of filming so that Brad would be ready in time for his next film, *Interview with a Vampire*. During filming, rumors were flying about their relationship. To counter the tabloids, Brad explained the problem: "I didn't want my character to show his cards so blatantly, and Ed did. So, you got two people who care about the film and the character and we had different views. Fortunately, something good is going to be squeezed out of that."

In fact, Brad was entirely supportive of *Legends* and its director—until he saw the final cut. Scenes that Brad felt essential to Tristan's redemption were cut. He was disappointed because he believed the film no longer portrayed the truth about Tristan's struggle to retain his sanity.

Zwick claimed the scenes were cut to develop the other characters. But his explanation didn't cut it with Brad. In a rare moment, Brad spoke out: "By taking out so much as they did, the movie becomes too mushy, 'cause there's no space between the mush. If I'd known where it was going to end up, I would have really fought against the cheese. The Kraft macaroni dinner." Not wanting to arouse controversy or hurt feelings, he backtracked, placing the blame on his own performance: "The movie's not cheesy by any means. There are moments where, if reduced to that, if that's all we were going to see of him, I would have whittled it down. I wouldn't have shown so much."

Interview with a Vampire (1994)

Watching the film must have been extremely upsetting for Brad, who had, his whole life, been looking for the reality he saw to be reflected back at him accurately. Brad didn't see the world through rose-colored glasses. He didn't see life as mushy, and he didn't see it covered in cheese. And he worked from the deepest parts of himself, which was difficult and draining, in order to portray a more truthful existence. For what? The cutting-room floor.

> **Responding to Brad's criticism, Zwick said, "Our process was not without tensions, passions. Brad has great artistic impulses, great instincts. But in the acting world, he skipped a lot of steps. He's no less emotional, but he's less obviously expressive, and the role required real self-revealment. Where he's from, you keep that to yourself."**

Straight from the physically and emotionally exhausting filming of *Legends*, Brad arrived in Louisiana for six more months of exhaustive work. Making *Interview with a Vampire* was hardly pleasant for him. After filming wrapped, Brad said, "I hated doing this movie. Hated it. I loved watching it. Completely hated doing it. My character was depressed from beginning to end. Five and a half months of that is too much."

Interview with a Vampire is the first in a series of baroque novels that follow the stories of various vampire characters throughout history. This novel follows the story of Louis de Ponte du Lac, a 19th-century plantation owner. After the death of his family, Louis sinks into despair. He crosses paths with the vampire Lestat, who promises him release from his earthly suffering. Louis gives in but discovers being a vampire offends his morality so much that his anguish is even deeper than when he was alive.

The history of this 1976 bestselling novel becoming a film is as baroque and twisted as the story it tells. The book was optioned before it was published, and yet it took 18 years for the film version to appear, a year longer than *Legends*. It would seem that the

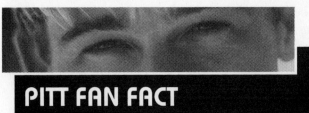

PITT FAN FACT

Brad later admitted he'd never finished reading the novel *Interview with a Vampire*.

Hollywood machine moves slowly. At the time the book was first optioned, Paramount thought the market was already flooded with vampire movies, including *Dracula* and *Love at First Bite*, and decided to wait for Anne Rice to complete the sequel. The studio reasoned that the two novels could be rolled into one movie. The problem was that the sequel wasn't published until 1985, and Paramount didn't care for it. It dropped its option, which was picked up by Lorimar Television, and when Warner Brothers purchased Lorimar, the rights to both books were passed on to the studio.

In 1989, David Geffen, who loved the book and had a production deal with Warner Brothers, took on the role of producer. True to his reputation of doing business unconventionally, Geffen threw out all previous scripts and commissioned Ann Rice to write the screenplay. In Hollywood, authors of optioned books are rarely hired to write their own screenplay. There are good reasons for this. Authors are often too attached to their material to treat it for the screen. Wanting to control the outcome, they can be notoriously vocal about the treatment their novels receive. Ann Rice was thrilled to be asked, and she happily accepted. True to Hollywood's perceptions of authors, Rice had strong opinions and was unreserved in sharing them. To be fair, Rice's attachment to this novel may have been stronger than was usual. She wrote it while mourning the cruel death of her five-year-old daughter, who had died from leukemia.

Rice had three suggestions for the director she'd prefer Geffen to hire: Canadian director David Cronenberg (*The Fly, Naked Lunch*), English director Ridley Scott (*Alien, Thelma and Louise*) or Irish director Neil Jordan (*Company of Wolves, The Crying*

Game). Her choices were all acclaimed directors who were known for films with elements of fantasy, horror and the grotesque—suitable for a dark and moody film about vampires. Geffen hired Jordan on the strength of his work in *The Crying Game*—an art-house film that became a blockbuster hit. Also nominated for Best Picture and Best Director, *The Crying Game* had earned Jordan an Oscar for Best Screenplay.

Rice's delight at Neil Jordan being hired to direct her film quickly became a series of public battles. Jordan rewrote the screenplay that Ann Rice had submitted. He said frankly, "The story didn't work—nobody got the script right—so I had to get the script to work, to make it kind of beautiful." A good film is simple; it focuses on a single theme and everything that happens in the film illuminates this theme, which comes from the main character's central conflict. The theme takes the specific conflict and expands it so that it becomes relevant to an audience. Jordan had to find the simplicity: "I had to bring the moral dilemma to the forefront, Louis's whole question of 'is he evil or is he good? Or is he beyond evil?'" Jordan worked meticulously with Rice's novel and screenplay to draw out the necessary cinematic elements, but despite his work, the final screenplay credit went entirely to Ann Rice.

The next clash was over casting, which was within Jordan's, and to a lesser extent, Geffen's authority. Jordan knew exactly which actor he wanted for the haunted Louis: Brad Pitt. "I saw everything he'd done, and he is just absolutely captivating," Jordan said of his choice. It was the casting of Lestat that created an uproar that continued throughout the production. Jordan's choice was strange, but it was his choice to make. Tom Cruise was cast to play the devilish and unrepentant Lestat. Jordan said of Cruise,

Jordan and Geffen felt it was best not to engage Rice in a press war, and besides, she had unwittingly helped ensure the film a great opening because of the controversy.

Interview with a Vampire (1994)

"It's just that the guy is so amazing." If Cruise wanted the part and was willing to take it all the way, then Jordan was thrilled.

Fans of the book were not thrilled. How could Cruise, who represented to the public success, the smiling, happy all-American good guy, play a creature of the night, the subversive symbol of underdogs, who were Rice's fans? Rice felt compelled to enter the fray publicly. In an interview with *The Los Angeles Times*, she said, "I was particularly stunned by the casting of Cruise. He is no more my vampire Lestat than Edward G. Robinson is Rhett Butler…I am puzzled as to why Cruise would want to take on the role. He's a cute kid, on top of the world, and on his way to becoming a great actor, but I'm not sure he knows what he's getting himself into. He should do himself a favor and withdraw."

> Her remarks were more than a little patronizing. Cruise was no "cute kid." He was the biggest movie star of his generation, and his position at the top didn't just happen. He was also an astute businessman. Accepting the role of Lestat was a calculated risk, one from which he would never walk away, no matter what Rice had to say.

Jordan and Geffen felt it was best not to engage Rice in a press war, and besides, she had unwittingly helped ensure the film a great opening because of the controversy.

The last snag in the production was not a trifling matter of clashing egos, but a heartbreaking tragedy. River Phoenix, who was cast in the role of the interviewer, collapsed on the sidewalk outside the Johnny Depp's nightclub, The Viper Room, and died of a drug overdose. Whereas Tom Cruise was the movie star of his generation, River Phoenix was the actor. Brad said, "I knew River a little, but I wanted to know him more. His death affected everyone on the movie, but at the same time, it was real personal. You gotta realize, River did a role in *My Own Private Idaho* that took it to a level that none of these other young guys have gotten to yet. I was really looking forward to him being on the set. It just seems like when we lost him, we all lost something special." In a heartfelt gesture, Christian Slater, who stepped into Phoenix's role, donated his salary to Phoenix's favorite charities.

Phoenix's death contributed, in part, to Brad's funk. But it was mostly playing the tortured character of Louis that made Brad so unhappy. For the first time in his career, Brad was taken over by his character. Some actors believe in submersing themselves in every aspect of their character; Brad likes more separation between himself and his characters: "Somewhere in the third or fourth week, you respond to things a little differently, like your character would respond. I don't like it. I can't wait to get my own clothes back on, listen to some good music, eat what I want to eat." Playing Louis affected Brad in a way he'd never been affected before. Neil Jordan thought it was because Brad and Louis were so alike: deeply empathetic and emotional.

Tabloids reported rumors of on-set conflicts between Cruise and Pitt. Although they never fought, the co-stars remained distant from each other. Brad and Tom were simply too different as characters, as actors and as people. Whatever they thought about each other privately, they remained respectful of each other's work in the film.

Staying on top wasn't what Brad wanted: he wanted to become a better actor. He wanted to be like Sean Penn, not Tom Cruise.

But for Brad, Cruise was the kind of actor Brad didn't want to become. A few months after the film finished shooting, Brad said, "I tell you the machine Tom runs is quite impressive. I wouldn't want to live like that but still…Listen, if you want to stay on top, you gotta stay on top." Staying on top wasn't what Brad wanted: he wanted to become a better actor. He wanted to be like Sean Penn, not Tom Cruise.

Filming two epics back-to-back made it an exhausting year for Brad. At the end of it, he had this to say: "This last year, I've been as happy as I've ever been, been miserable, been genius, been humiliated, been congratulated, been put down—I mean, the whole gamut of emotions. That's a pretty amazing year. I value that. Extremes. And it's come from acting. The hardest thing is to make it look easy."

chapter 7

playing House

Once you walk into money, it separates you, and it separates the outside world's perception of you. That's what I'm afraid of.

To recover his energy, Brad took some well-deserved time off. He finished filming *Interview* in April 1994 and didn't start filming his next movie, *Se7en*, a gritty police thriller, until December. After eight years in Hollywood, Brad felt his career was truly launched, and that he could take some time for himself. He had good reason to feel safe: in November 1994, *Interview* opened with a box office take of more than $38 million, reaching number five on *Variety's* list of all-time biggest openings. The film's audience dropped off quickly, but still, the movie grossed a decent $105 million in the theaters. Two months later, *Legends* did even better. It remained the number-one film in the United States for four weeks. Brad had opened two blockbusters, so not only could he choose his projects, he had also attained movie star status. Less happy news for Brad was that *People* named him Sexiest Man Alive for 1994.

During his hiatus, Brad read a lot of scripts, but he had plenty to keep him busy outside of movies. While filming *Legends*, Brad had purchased a house, and not just any house, but a Craftsmen house. Built in 1910, it was built according to the tenets of the American Arts & Crafts style. The Arts & Crafts movement was an architectural style that fascinated Brad, and its basic principles inform his architectural esthetics even today. The Arts & Crafts movement was a reaction to the Industrial Revolution. Its practitioners felt that people were becoming increasingly separated from their own creativity and individualism. Increasingly, people were living in an environment created with shoddy machine-made goods. The Arts & Crafts movement sought to re-establish architecture with craftsmen, returning to an honesty and beauty in design not found in mass-produced items. Arguably America's greatest designer, Frank Lloyd Wright was a member of this style. The connection with Frank Lloyd Wright that Brad discovered in college deepened when he bought his house.

The style that developed from the movement was focused on the materials from which something is made. The focus inspired Brad, and he used it as in redesigning his house, a project that took many years. The house, as it was described by *Vanity Fair* journalist Johanna Schneller, was "studded with terraces and balconies, perfectly integrated into its many-acre site. At night, it looks like a crazy stack of shoeboxes, glowing with amber and burnt-orange light. There's a pool. There's a pond. There's a small man-made cave, which Pitt has furnished with an Oriental rug. There are 40-odd chameleons living in wooden Chinese lantern-shaped structures in the backyard." Besides the many-breeding chameleons, Brad was sharing his home with three mutts: Todd Potter, Saudi and Purty, named thus because "he is so damned purty."

His environment was important to him and continues to be so. Especially because his fame has made moving about anonymously impossible, Brad needed a home that allowed him time and space to relax in normalcy. "The home is very, very important, especially now as this thing builds and builds and gets completely out of hand," he said, talking about fame. Although he is not fond of fame, he is fond of furniture, especially if it's handmade. He can talk for

His need to do something real led him to choose the low-budget thriller co-starring Morgan Freeman over the big-budget *Apollo 13* co-starring Tom Hanks.

hours about the texture and grain of wood. When he speaks about design, he doesn't sound like a movie star: he uses words like *proportion*, *materials*, *light* and *perspective*.

Besides creating a haven for himself and his animal friends, Brad was choosing his next projects. First was the starring role of Detective David Mills in **Se7en**, then the featured role of Jeffrey Goines in **Twelve Monkeys**, followed by the role of Michael Sullivan in the ensemble piece, **Sleepers**. Making three movies back to back swallowed up the next year of his life.

Se7en appealed to Brad because, after the trio of *River*, *Legends* and *Interview*, he wanted to play something other than the pretty boy against the backdrop of a historical epic. Brad said of the *Se7en* script, "At first I thought it was just another cop-buddy flick, but upon reading it, I knew it was different. People are going to love it or hate it, but they'll be talking about it." His need to do something real led him to choose the low-budget thriller co-starring Morgan Freeman over the big-budget *Apollo 13* co-starring Tom Hanks.

Brad found what he was looking for in the gritty *Se7en*, which was as dark as a mainstream movie can be. The story begins as a police thriller with Detective David Mills, a keener recently transferred to the big city from his country posting, and his partner, William Somerset, a philosophical, burnt-out cop who is a week away from retirement, investigating a series of murders. The grotesque and cruel murders each represent one of the seven deadly sins. They are unable to crack the case until the killer turns himself in. The movie then shifts genres from police action to psychological horror, with David Mills at the center. The ending is not a happy one.

Se7en (1995)

The appeal of the unhappy ending to Brad and director David Fincher was the ambiguous moral context. As Fincher explained, "It builds and lulls you into thinking there is some kind of sense and order to things. And then the final act of the movie is revealed to contain just as much chaos as everyday life. That's a horrifying realization for an audience. It compromises their expectations of entertainment."

Producer Arnold Kopelson, who had brought such brave and successful films to the screen as *Platoon*, *The Fugitive* and *Falling Down*, hired David Fincher as the director of *Se7en*. A music video director who had worked with such luminaries as David Bowie, Fincher had ventured into film directing only once before, and that was for the film *Alien 3*. The producers were controlling, the script weak and the critics vicious. He intended *Alien 3* to be his first and last experience with film. Luckily, Kopelson was able to convince Fincher otherwise.

Fincher cast the role of Somerset easily. He wanted Morgan Freeman, and Freeman wanted to do the role. More difficult was casting the character of David Mills. Fincher first dismissed Brad as too pretty for the role, but when he heard the star was interested, he set up a meeting. Brad's enthusiasm changed his mind. Michael de Luca, head of production for New Line, said of Brad, "Brad helped to get this movie made. When he came aboard, people got a lot less insecure about the film. It was very brave of him. I love it when people go against type. To come off pictures like *Legends of the Fall* and *Interview with the Vampire* and play a homophobic, bigoted, neo-fascist cop with a crew cut—it was a very cool thing for Brad to do."

With Brad on board, Fincher was left with casting the actress that would play Brad's wife. Ironically, Brad suggested a 22-year-old actress whom he had met briefly several months before. That actress was Gwyneth Paltrow, and Brad had no idea where his innocent suggestion would lead. Gwyneth was already in Fincher's mind—he had seen her in a little-seen picture starring Meg Ryan and Dennis Quaid called *Flesh and Bone*, and he was impressed. Even though she was Fincher's first choice, he almost didn't bother to call her. Her reputation for being picky made him think there was no chance that she'd accept the part. Brad asked her to come and meet with Fincher, Kopelson and himself. Kopelson didn't know Gwyneth before the meeting, but as Fincher recalls, he was just as taken with her: "She came in and sat down for about two seconds and said, 'Do you have a rest room?' and she walked out of the room, and Arnold said, 'She's perfect...'"

Like Juliette Lewis, Gwyneth had parents who were in the business. Her father, Bruce Paltrow, was a television producer and director, best known for his TV show, *St. Elsewhere*. Her mother, Blythe Danner, is an award-winning theater actress, who also works in film and TV. And like Juliette, Gwyneth was nearly a decade younger than Brad, and both girls were born in L.A.—but that's where the similarities end. Whereas Juliette stayed in L.A., Gwyneth grew up in Manhattan, surrounded by her parents' friends, who were the makers of high culture. Juliette dropped out of high school three weeks after she began, and at the age of 14, she became legally emancipated from her parents. Gwyneth went to Spence School, the exclusive all-girls private school, and then on to the University of California, where she studied art history before dropping out to pursue a film career in 1991. Juliette and Gwyneth were very different in background, style and character.

To Brad, Gwyneth was perfect, and their romance began shortly after filming started. Brad said, "I knew immediately, I'll tell you that much. I got within 10 feet of her, and

To Brad, Gwyneth was perfect, and their romance began shortly after filming started.

I got goofy. I couldn't talk." For Gwyneth, it took a little longer—but not much. She recalled, "I don't think either of us was expecting love or looking for it, and it came as a shock to both of us. We went to an Italian restaurant in Los Angeles for a wonderful meal, and the romance grew from there. I was charmed by his intelligence and sensitivity, his closeness to his family and the way in which he was completely down to earth."

It hardly seems possible that romance could grow out of *Se7en*, with the movie's dark environment, its morally ambiguous theme and its portrayal of a chaotic world. But it did, and for once, Brad wholeheartedly enjoyed his job. Working with a director with whom he shared many sensibilities and a co-star like Morgan Freeman, generous and solid, made the job of acting less agonizing and much easier. It was filmed in 55 days because of Brad's schedule—a good, short, well-run shoot with only one major mishap, which unfortunately happened to be Brad's. "It happened during a scene where I'm chasing the bad guy, and traffic is jammed so I'm running across the hoods of cars. In the rain," he recalled. "I was trying the do-your-own-stunt thing. You know, that Joe Mannix approach? And I bit it. Hard. Basically, it was a matter of me trying to be cool and failing miserably. I slipped right through the car window. I wore a cast for the rest of the film. I did a lot of pocket acting."

Pocket acting seemed to work because **Se7en** garnered Brad great reviews. More important, the film found an audience. It was incredibly successful at the box office, eventually grossing approximately $350 million.

Next up for Brad was *Twelve Monkeys* in which he played a small but pivotal role, a role unlike any he had played before. Directed by Terry Gilliam, a member of the Monty Python gang, *Twelve Monkeys* was based on a 1963 surreal short film called *La Jetée* by Chris Marker. This sci-fi action film plays on the theme of madness, questioning whether the main character James Cole, played by Bruce Willis, is mad or whether the story he tells Kathryn Railly, a psychiatrist played by Madeline Stowe, is true. As Cole tells it, a virus breaks out in 1996, causing worldwide devastation. He is from the year 2035, and he has traveled back in time to stop the outbreak of the virus. The suspect is Jeffery Goines, played by Brad, the righteous animal rights activist, whom Cole meets in the psychiatric ward.

For the role, Brad actually did research for his character, something of which he was usually suspicious. But because he was playing a character with bi-polar disorder, he wanted his portrayal to be accurate and having this mental illness was not something he could conjure up in his imagination. He went to Philadelphia, where the film was shooting, two weeks before he

Twelve Monkeys (1995)

was called so that he could attend daily group therapy sessions with bi-polar patients. Through his observation, he created a kind of lexicon of gestures, which later became his character Jeffery Goines.

"Brad Pitt really wanted to do the film. In many ways we were lucky because he was running away from the Sexiest-Man-in-the-World image," remarked Gilliam, "so he went in the opposite direction, and he certainly won't win that award for this film. People are going to realize how funny he is. His comic timing is wonderful. It's just funny stuff he's doing, and he comes across as absolutely crazy." Jeffery Goines was a showy part, perfect for a character actor, and more and more Brad was convinced his talents were best used, not as a leading man, but as a character actor. Alan Pakula, who directed Brad in *The Devil's Own* offered more insight into this paradox: "He says he's a character actor, and I know exactly what he means. Unlike many comparable big stars, especially of his generation, he takes chances. He does not just play a star persona. He tries to develop characters that are not obviously related to him, and in that way, he's just a very serious committed actor. At the same time, there is something about Brad that is deeply sympathetic, aside from the fact that he's so obviously attractive." David Fincher agrees completely with Pakula's assessment. He's amazed that Brad's looks haven't stopped him from having a serious career in movies.

Between filming *Se7en* and *Twelve Monkeys*, Brad and Gwyneth made their relationship public. Unfortunately, it was more public that they intended. On April 28, 1994, the pair had their first public outing, attending the London premiere of *Legends of the Fall*. Instantly, the gorgeous, golden duo captured the imagination of press, who elevated Brad and Gwyneth to the mythical status of *the* Hollywood couple. Sadly, this violation of privacy devastated Brad—it profoundly offended his sense of fair play. After the opening, the two flew to St. Barts for a brief stint of sun and fun—a little time together before Brad started *Twelve Monkeys*. They had chosen the most private place they could for their stay. While they were there, enjoying some nude sunbathing, a journalist with a telephoto lens snapped pictures and sold them to British tabloid *Celebrity Sleuth*. Eventually, the photos made their way to the Internet, making private moments of the couple all too public. Brad called the invasion of privacy "stalking," and he felt they had been violated. But Brad being

Sleepers (1996)

Brad, he didn't want to make too much fuss about it. Having attained such a privileged place in society, he was cautious about saying anything negative about the challenges fame had brought him. Still, he took to lobbing eggs at a tour bus that came by his home every Sunday. And when the eggs didn't work, he planted trees to give him privacy from the people peering at him from a tour bus. His relaxed attitude about the St. Barts photos, however, came back to haunt him—at the worst time he could imagine.

> When the lovebirds returned from St. Barts, Brad moved into Gwyneth's Greenwich Village apartment. His next project was being filmed in New York, so the move was ideal. Of course, he kept his L.A. dream home, but the ease with which he moved in with Gwyneth was remarkable considering his hesitance to move in with Juliette.

After *Twelve Monkeys*, Brad's next project was *Sleepers*, an adaptation of the controversial book written by Lorenzo Carcaterra. At first, simply a bestselling novel, *Sleepers* tells the haunting tale of four kids from Hell's Kitchen who do time in a juvenile reformatory after a street vendor almost dies during a prank involving his hot dog cart. While serving their one-year sentence, the four boys are sexually and sadistically abused by a guard named Sean Nokes. Fifteen years later and now grown up, two of the four meet up with Nokes and shoot him dead. The other two are pulled into the case and manipulate the trial in order to serve justice. Renowned director Barry Levinson (*Diner*, *Rain Man*) had gathered an incredible cast of actors, with Brad, Jason Patric, Ron Eldard, Billy Crudup playing the grownup boys and Dustin Hoffman, Robert DeNiro and Kevin Bacon rounding out the cast.

What made *Sleepers* so controversial was that Carcaterra claimed that his book wasn't a novel at all, but a non-fiction account of what had happened to him and his friends. All he did, he claimed, was change the names and locations to protect the identity of those involved. But if *Sleepers* is a true tale, then two men got away with murder because a Catholic priest committed perjury. In the time of the OJ Simpson trial, such mockery of the justice system was hard to swallow. After the New York legal community researched old cases extensively and could not find any case resembling the events of his book, Carcaterra refused to discuss the discrepancy. Because of his silence and because no evidence could be found to corroborate his story, the book is largely considered a work of fiction.

Movie reviewers took up the fact or fiction question, which was too bad. True or not, the movie told a good story. Most reviewers were impressed by the quality of acting. Brad had done well yet again.

Brad took Gwyneth home to Missouri to meet his parents. There, they spent Christmas of 1995 in peace and quiet, before Brad was off to wrap *Sleepers* in January. The new year was off to a great start with *Twelve Monkeys* opening in the number-one spot, and Brad receiving a Golden Globe nomination for his performance in the film. He was madly in love, and he had two new movies, *The Devil's Own* and *Seven Years in Tibet* on the go.

chapter 8

Climbing Mountains

Loss is one step behind death…

For Brad, 1996 began with promise. Attending the Golden Globe awards with Gwyneth, Brad was blown away to hear his name spoken as the recipient as Best Supporting Actor award for his work in *Twelve Monkeys*. Seemingly unprepared, Brad stumbled through his acceptance speech, thanking the people in his professional and personal life. He gushed about having Gwyneth in his life, calling her "my angel, the love of my life."

Winning a Golden Globe is no small honor. The Hollywood Foreign Press Association, whose membership is made up of respected entertainment journalists from around the world, hosts the awards. The internal Hollywood politics that play out in the Academy Awards are not so evident in the Golden Globes' selections. The Golden Globes, however, are considered the best indicator of which actors and films will be nominated for the Academy Awards. True to form, Brad was nominated for an Oscar in the Best Supporting Actor category. Losing out to Kevin Spacey, who won for his incredible performance in *The Usual Suspects*, Brad said of the Academy Awards and choosing roles geared towards them: "It's a crap shoot. It's got to be personal in each film. If it sinks, it sinks, and if it floats, good for you, because I just don't put a lot of emphasis on it. Sure it would be flattering, but most of the time I disagree with their choices."

Strangely, though Brad pursued stardom, he's uncomfortable with the positive public attention that comes from being a star. He's had to fight feelings of

> He starts from nothing, and nothing is a place of vulnerability from which all good acting comes.

unworthiness each time he steps onto a new set. Being nominated for these awards embarrassed Brad; he felt there were other actors who were more deserving. Although he enjoyed attending the ceremonies, particularly because he was with Gwyneth, he would prefer to avoid them altogether.

Brad isn't pulling out false modesty for the sake of the press; he is showing his unflinching honesty. Brad understands that movie stars are replaceable—when one actor passes on a role, another will take it and make it his own. Brad's a thinker, and the nature of stardom is a subject he has thought about deeply. "I've had it easy. Too easy," Brad said, reflecting on his status. "I'm starting to believe that anyone who's successful in these little circles has got to feel that. That's why a lot of them don't make it. You know, people want to be famous. You have no idea what you're getting into." Paradoxically, Brad's feelings of unworthiness are a sign of his talent. These feelings mean that each time he begins a role, he doesn't repeat what has worked for him before. He starts from nothing, and nothing is a place of vulnerability from which all good acting comes.

In February 1996, Brad began to film *The Devil's Own*, and the promise of a "golden year" was broken. To unravel the truth of what happened over the six months of filming is difficult. The truth exists somewhere between tabloids reports of a skyrocketing budget, a burgeoning production schedule, ego clashes, script rewrites and the cast and crew's refusal to acknowledge any troubles.

Initially, *The Devil's Own* was a project that excited Brad. Written by Kevin Jarre, the screenplay itself was enough for Brad to attach himself to the project as an unknown in 1991. In 1994, he was the first actor signed when the project went into pre-production.

The Devil's Own (1997)

By the time filming began, Brad said, "The script that I had loved was gone." He was right—the original script was discarded, and the new script went through at least seven complete rewrites under director Alan Pakula. Rumor has it that the film was rewritten to boost Harrison Ford's character from supporting to leading role. "I guess people just had different visions, and you can't argue with that," Brad said, diplomatically. "But then I wanted out, and the studio head said, 'All right, we'll let you out, but it'll be $63 million for starters.'" After his unsuccessful attempt to leave the production, Brad

came back and made the film with dedicated professionalism, even though script changes were a daily occurrence, and the production ran over by two months causing Brad's next project to be delayed.

> In **The Devil's Own**, Brad plays an Irish Republican gunman named Frankie McGuire, who comes to the U.S. to purchase weapons for his cause. A sympathetic Irish-American judge sets McGuire up with an assumed identity and a place to stay—the home of Tom O'Meara, played by Harrison Ford. O'Meara is a by-the-books policeman. Even so, the two men bond and develop a friendship. Slowly, O'Meara discovers McGuire's identity and is faced with a tough decision.

Brad landed himself in hot water after the film wrapped. While on location for *Seven Years in Tibet*, Brad gave a surprisingly candid interview with *Newsweek*. He called the film a "disaster," and said "it was the most irresponsible bit of filmmaking—if you can even call it that—that I've ever seen. I couldn't believe it." His statement caused quite a stir at the studio, and after Brad received several calls, he made a public clarification that same day. Remembering the furor, Brad said, "Man, that got stinky didn't it? I didn't clarify—it was my fault—I was talking about pre-production time, which was chaos to me. Once we got in, we fought for the movie. I'm very happy with it, and I've clarified that."

Sadly, all the struggle and script changes didn't make *The Devil's Own* a good movie. They didn't make the movie Brad envisioned. He stated, "The goal of the movie was to have two good men who come from relatively the same place and thinking.

They become tight along the way as they get to know each other. But eventually, their beliefs cause a clash, and they have to address it." Instead, the movie confused the premise and no one escaped the wrath of the reviewers. The confusion stemmed from whether Brad's character was meant to be the villain or merely that of an anti-hero. As Roger Ebert said, "Either way, the film should make it clear whether it considers the Brad Pitt character to be a hero or villain. My best guess is he's a villain given a moral touch-up because he's also a movie star." Universally panned, a few reviewers even said that *The Devil's Own* shows all that's wrong with Hollywood.

> In August, Brad headed to Argentina, where the first five months of *Seven Years in Tibet* was filmed. Although he was far from home, he was much happier on the set in Argentina than he had been in New York filming *The Devil's Own*—mostly because he wasn't alone. "Gwynnie was with me the whole time. It was excellent. You put in a hard day, then you come home and...there she is. She's sunshine. She sure is."

Seven Years in Tibet was taken from the autobiography of Austrian mountaineer Heinrich Harrer, who was on a mountain-climbing expedition when World War II broke out. Captured and imprisoned by the Allies, he and fellow climber Peter Aufschnaiter managed to escape. They found refuge in Lhasa, the holy city of Tibetan Buddhists—a place that had not allowed foreigners to enter until Harrer and Aufschnaiter arrived. Harrer became the tutor of the Dalai Lama until, at age 21, the Dalai Lama was forced to flee to India. Harrer's story had remarkable significance when he made his way back west. He had witnessed the oppression of the Tibetans under Chinese rule and was the first Westerner to bring worldwide awareness of the Tibetans' plight. French director Jean-Jacques Annaud (*The Bear*, *Name of the Rose*) found Harrer's journey similar to Brad's: "I think this movie means a lot to Brad. People still perceive him as a good-looking teenager. I think he is fighting for self-respect. It's about his professional honesty."

Harrer was a complex character, neither hero nor villain. He had abandoned his wife and child to pursue his obsession with mountain climbing and yet, through his relationship with the Dalai Lama, he begins a journey of redemption. Many actors vied for the part, including Richard Gere, who had been considered for the part of Harrer in the mid-1980s when the project began. But, by the 1990s, Gere's career had faded and the search for the star continued. Annaud (*The Bear*, *Name of the Rose*) chose Brad because he was absolutely charmed by him. And besides, "I found it comforting that he not only understood what it was about, but it was also about something that he wanted to sort out for his own life: fame and success versus respect and self-respect," Annaud said. "I was thrilled to see that he had so many common grounds with the real Heinrich Harrer, who, by the way, was an extremely appealing man. He was very physical, and at the same time, became a writer. I didn't look any further, Brad became Harrer to me, and that was the beginning and end of it."

Originally, the film was to be shot in India, but under pressure from the Chinese government, the country refused to let the production film there.

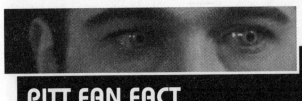

Filming was mainly done in Argentina for four months and in Canada for five. In Argentina, the location was near a tiny town with two streets and a population of 250 people. Even there, Brad could not get away from his fame. Annaud recalls the change in the town when Brad arrived. Inviting him to the local restaurant for dinner, Annaud recalled, "Well, that day was known as 'Brad's arrival,' and there were about 1000 young girls waiting and climbing on top of the building. All the while, I was reinstating to Brad the world of serenity—that the movie is about a man in love with his inner self. It was hilarious and frightening at the same time."

Still, Brad's fame was so large that it caused problems like disrupting filming, not to mention going way over budget on security spending. David Thewlis, Brad's co-star, recalled, "I could go to a bar and hang out, but he couldn't even do that without causing a riot." He was impressed with how down-to-earth Brad was.

Brad was honored to work with Thewlis, a British actor whom Brad called "the greatest actor of my generation." Before shooting began, the two met up to learn the basics of mountain climbing by going on an introductory expedition in Italy—an experience that completely hooked Brad. "All your tendons are shaking, and you don't think you're going to make it, but somehow you get over it," he said. "It's definitely a lesson in fear and knowing who you are."

In between shooting in Argentina and Canada, Brad and Gwyneth announced their engagement in December of 1996. Brad spent months designing Gwyneth's ring, and when it was ready, he proposed. That he would get married and start a family was never a question for Brad. The question was who was the right girl, and Gwyneth seemed to be the answer. The truth is that underneath his bohemian lifestyle, Brad valued such conventions as marriage and family. At age 33, he was ready. "I can't wait, man," he said about getting hitched. "Walking down the aisle, wear the ring, kiss the bride. Oh, it's going to be great. Marriage is an amazing thing. And what a compliment: 'You're the one I want to spend the rest of my life with,' you know? Because I'm only going to do it once."

In British Columbia, where the mountain-climbing scenes were filmed, Brad was extraordinarily content. Describing the process of filming, Brad said, "We all pile into these helicopters. You take off in these little tin cans, and you fight the wind, trying to stay level. You fly up these mountains and land on a frozen lake, this wall of blue ice glowing. It's fantastic. The minute the safety guy says, 'We gotta go,' we dump everything, stop shooting, everybody gets in the helicopter and we go down."

Once again, for Brad, Canadian weather wasn't cooperating. BC was having a particularly temperate winter, and the rapidly changing weather kept stalling the shoot because of safety concerns. Brad wasn't bothered; here in the seclusion of the mountains, there were, for once, no screaming fans. He didn't mind that the film was over-running because he was enjoying the experience so much. "There's nothing to do but work and eat," he said. "If only it could always be like this." The only thing missing for him was his girl, Gwynnie.

a Charlie Brown Year

i'm the guy who's got everything. I know. But I'm telling you, once you got everything, then you're just left yourself. I've said it before, and I'll say it again: It doesn't help you sleep better, and you don't wake up better because of it.

In hindsight, the time in Canada provided Brad with the strength he needed when, in the summer of 1997, one by one, a series of events threatened his fragile happiness.

First was the revelation that Harrer, who was 84 years old in 1997, had been a member of the Nazi party. A German magazine, *Stern,* published an article that accused Harrer of not only being a member of the SS, but also of joining that organization as early as 1933, when it was still illegal in Austria. The article ran with a photograph of Hitler congratulating Harrer on an expedition. Many people were outraged that Hollywood would produce a movie about such a man—not because he was believed to have participated in any crimes against humanity, but because he had not disclosed the fact of his membership in his autobiography, in which he criticizes China's treatment of Tibet. To the press, Harrer claimed a clear conscience.

After his involvement with *The Devil's Own*, Brad wasn't looking for another commotion. Still, he tackled the issue as it came up in interviews. "I met Harrer, who is now in his 80s, and liked him," Brad said. "I didn't ask him a thing about his past, because I felt inhibited about playing someone living." In a moment of openness, Brad admitted, "Would I have taken the part if I'd known the truth? Probably not, because I'd have looked at the story and the man a whole new way." The controversy didn't draw moviegoers to the theater, however. *Seven*

Years in Tibet was never meant to be a big money-maker, but its terrible box office take was a disappointment to all involved—all that hard work creating an epic of social importance for very few people. Critics were more generous, although not entirely enthusiastic. Succinctly, Peter Travers of *Rolling Stone* summed up the general view of the film: "*Seven Years in Tibet,* however flawed, has feeling and purpose. It bears witness."

Next, and shocking enough to capture headlines in mainstream press, Brad and Gwyneth broke off their engagement. Because the couple had become the model of perfect Hollywood love, the split was entirely unexpected. Everyone wanted to know why they had suddenly split, but neither Brad nor Gwyneth gave a reason. The press went wild speculating, and tabloids published every piece of gossip that came up. That Brad was a womanizer and Gwyneth had had enough was the one story that stuck. However, Paltrow was quick to dispel the rumors. In a press conference, she said, "The desperation to uncover a reason why has produced information that is false, unfair and foolish. Not only is Brad Pitt beyond reproach, but he is a man of extreme integrity and goodness." Brad's long-time makeup artist and friend, Jean Black, also spoke out on the matter of Brad's fidelity. She said, "When Brad's in love, his loyalty and commitment is beyond reproach. Despite what the press says about him stepping out or whatever, in the eight years I've known him, I've never seen that side of him."

As for Brad, he was cryptic about the reasons for their breakup. Whatever the reasons were, he was depressed, disillusioned and deeply disappointed about the subject. Unlike with Juliette, Brad had no interest in pursuing a friendship with Gwyneth, saying only, "It's over." Shortly after the breakup, Brad was unusually brusque: "This is just real world, and I'm growing up. Life is tough, and

"Being in movies doesn't make you laugh any harder or cry any less."

it's crooked, but it's pretty fantastic. Moments like this go in circles, and it's just when you get comfortable that something's going to mess you up." As time passed, he became increasingly dismissive of Gwyneth, referring to the time he had spent with her as the "Paltrow period."

With remarkable insight, producer Paul Feldsher, a close friend of Brad's, shared his perspective on the two. He pointed out their differences: Gwyneth's love of the limelight versus Brad's love of home and how those differences, at first, contributed to their happiness. But eventually, Brad's midwestern sensibilities and Gwyneth's Manhattan sophistication led to tension between them. It isn't hard to imagine that Brad's desire for authenticity and Gwyneth's pretensions would eventually cause conflicts. In this light, Brad and Gwyneth made a brave and mature decision not to stay together.

Brad and Gwyneth parted in June. Cruelly, in August, the St. Barts pictures of the two of them surfaced again. This time, however, they were published in *Playgirl* magazine, and this time, Brad was angry enough to sue. His argument was plain—journalists covered newsworthy events—as he pointed out, "And the fact that Brad Pitt has a penis and here's proof—it's not news. It's not needed." Winning his lawsuit meant that *Playgirl* had to stop distribution, recall the magazines it had distributed, and destroy all the issues that featured the St. Barts photos.

Brad described this period as his "Charlie Brown year." In his interview with Diane Sawyer, she pressed him to explain what he meant. He replied, "It means you can have the best intentions, but you're still going to end up with rocks in your Halloween bag, you know? You just have periods where, you know, your number's not coming up. Things aren't working right. I just call it the Charlie Brown year."

> "People have much worse years, and people survive....It's just when you don't think you—you're not sure you can take much more, you know? You find something. And you get over that hump."

Brad had one more hump to face—the most devastating of all—and that was the heart pains his father suffered while visiting his son on the Rhode Island set of *Meet Joe Black*. Rushed to a hospital in Boston, Bill Pitt was eventually diagnosed with a "heart irregularity." Although his father was well enough, Brad had to face that some day, his life would no longer include his father. As Brad has often said, being a movie star doesn't get you a ticket out of dealing with all the ups and downs, and triumph and grief that life hands us: "Being in movies doesn't make you laugh any harder or cry any less."

While Brad was dealing with concerns about his father, Gwyneth, *Playgirl* and the brouhaha over *The Devil's Own* and *Seven Years in Tibet*, he was filming *Meet Joe Black*, the third in his series of film flops. An epic—a leisurely-paced two hours and 45 minutes—*Meet Joe Black* tells the story of publishing tycoon Bill Parrish, played by Anthony Hopkins, who opens the door to Death one night. The two strike a deal: Death will delay Parrish's departure, while Parrish teaches Death the wonders of living. Parrish introduces Death as Joe Black to his daughter, and the two share

As Brad asked, "Here's the first problem: who the hell is Death? Where are you going to go for your research?"

Meet Joe Black (1998)

a brief love affair. The film is made up mostly of long scenes of dialogue between two characters particularly Parrish and Black. While Anthony Hopkins shines—his classical theatrical training makes wordiness captivating, Brad falters. But acting abilities aside, the idea is to blame—Parrish is a flesh-and-blood character, whereas Black is a literary construct. Death, after all, isn't a character, but a concept. As Brad asked, "Here's the first problem: who the hell is Death? Where are you going to go for your research?"

Brad, forever unsure about his abilities as an actor, has often said that the worse his state of mind is, the worse his performance is. During the filming of *Meet Joe Black*, Brad couldn't have been is a worse state. "It's funny. Movies come along, and you're in a particular place in your life—this is not an excuse—but it always colors your performance, I find. I can't watch a film without knowing where I was then, what little terrain of life I was going through at that point," he said, reflecting on the film. "I mean most of the things I've done I'd love to have a second shot at. With this one, I think I made mistakes in it, but fortunately, the film is bigger than my mistakes." Brad credits the movie's success in dealing with such poignant themes of loss to the director, writer and the performance of Anthony Hopkins.

When *Meet Joe Black* was released a year after it had wrapped, Brad found that reviewers echoed his personal view of his work, but the echoes were harsher and crueler. To these reviews, Brad said, "I just figured it was my turn. Listen, I didn't agree with most of it. I like the pace of *Meet Joe Black*. I think it got a little too long-winded. But so what? It's not infallible. It's art. I don't think it deserves a beating from people who don't make things."

In the year between the film's shooting and its release, Brad hunkered down, away from the press. In interviews, after he surfaced, Brad had changed—he seemed more paranoid and less willing to play the entertainment game. For example, he believed that *Meet Joe Black* failed to capture the imaginations of reviewers and audiences because of him, and not because of his abilities, but because of what he represented. He told a journalist, "If Marty [Brest, the director] had made the same movie with someone else, it wouldn't have got the flogging it got. Because, look, I represent the guy whose got everything. I deserve a beating, you know what I'm saying?"

The self-professed mushy guy even beat up on love: "As we're going into the 21st century, I think we're far enough along—we know enough now, that no one can save you. I go crazy when I read a script and one character says, 'I can't live without you.' It drives me crazy. Because we're teaching the wrong thing." Asked if he believed in happily ever after, he replied, "No, there is no such thing." At the time he made these observations, he was falling in love. But for first time, his love was realistic, shaped by his past experiences. He understood that love was hard work, and it took a lot more than love to make a relationship work or an individual happy.

After a year of soul searching and self reflection, Brad did some growing up and figuring out: "I think of the pain I've felt in my life…pain is relative but…the Paltrow period was a truly valuable time for me personally." A great learning experience, the end of his relationship forced him to sit down and evaluate it. He needed to know what went wrong so that he wouldn't make those mistakes again. Two major events also happened that shaped who is Brad today. First, he started dating Jennifer Aniston, and

…he turned to Norton and said, "I'll never be in a better movie than that."

second, he filmed *Fight Club*, the polar opposite in sentiment to *Meet Joe Black*.

Unlike previous relationships that had started on set, the stars' managers had set them up. Brad, a self-sworn TV junkie, was a huge fan of *Friends*, the show in which Jennifer starred. And Jennifer had seen and liked most of Brad's movies. Like Juliette and Gwyneth, Jennifer had TV connections through her father, who played Victor Kiriakis on *Days of Our Lives*. Jennifer began training as an actress when she attended the New York's High School of the Performing Arts. After a couple of off-Broadway shows, she moved to L.A. to pursue a movie career. Instead, she found fame in TV with the hit series *Friends* as the vacuous Rachel Green. Throughout the run of *Friends*, Jennifer began building acclaim for her performances in low-budget film such as *The Good Girl*.

> Recognizing they had something good, Brad and Jennifer were protective of their budding relationship. They did whatever they could to keep it from the press until they were sure of what they had. As Brad put it, "We did well for a while there. We just didn't participate. We just wanted to see if something was going to grow on its own without any outside influence. We just wanted to keep it ours."

Besides appearing as himself—or the flat, narcissistic version of himself—in *Being John Malkovich*, Brad worked on only one film during this period: *Fight Club*. It was a film that meant so much to him that when he first saw it with co-star Edward Norton, he turned to Norton and said, "I'll never be in a better movie than that." *Fight Club,* which was adapted from the scathing and satirical debut novel of Chuck Palahniuk, was the first movie that Brad was involved in that was a social commentary.

Fight Club (1999)

As a child, Brad's favorite movie, *Planet of the Apes,* presented a social commentary on religion. With *Fight Club,* he had the opportunity to make a movie in the same vein—just a different society and a different generation. Whereas *Reality Bites,* directed by Ben Stiller, looked at Generation X in a light comedy about young folks who were a little lost and lax, *Fight Club,* directed by David Fincher, looked at Generation X in a black comedy about angry, adult men whose rage and powerlessness were no longer being extinguished by consumerism.

Played by Edward Norton, the film's narrator, whose name is never used, is a thirty-something desk jockey. He's successful in the sense that he can buy the latest IKEA trinket and fill his fridge with condiments, but in order to feel alive, he attends support groups for people dying from cancer. Traveling for his work, he meets Tyler Durden, a soap manufacturer, on an airplane. They strike up a conversation, and by the end of the trip, the buttoned-down narrator has made a crazy new friend and guru, who teaches him that the key to living might be found in destroying. One exercise in destruction they try is beating each other up, which leads to euphoria for them. Their injuries attract the interest of others, which leads to the creation of a formal fight club.

Soon fight clubs pop up everywhere, and it seems as though there just might be enough energy to destroy the corporate, consumerist culture that has made Generation X deteriorate.

Fight Club also reunited Brad with his *Se7en* director David Fincher with whom he shared many of the same aesthetics and perspectives. When Fincher called Brad about playing Tyler, Brad was so ecstatic about the project, Fincher quipped, "I hung up the phone, and he was knocking on my door in, like four minutes. And I live in a gated community. I don't know how he got past security."

"Finch is hyperbolizing the moment a little," Brad said in reply, "but yeah, I was pretty excited about doing it. I hadn't read anything like it, and I read everything. It's an astounding, extraordinary movie. It's a pummeling of information. It's a Mr. Fincher Opus. It's provocative, but thank God, it's provocative. People are hungry for films like this, films that make them think."

Fight Club (1999)

Unfortunately, when it comes to angry and intelligent films like *Fight Club*, people don't understand that they're meant to think. They react to the film, rather than think about its larger message. Slated for release in July 1999 opposite Stanley Kubrick's *Eyes Wide Shut*, *Fight Club* was put on hold for three months because of the shootings at Columbine. In April, two teenagers, dressed in black trench coats, went on a shooting spree at their school in Colorado. The collective horror surrounding the event created a backlash against Hollywood as the manufacturer of teen violence. And when *Fight Club* opened, many reviewers were offended. Roger Ebert called it "a thrill ride masquerading as philosophy," and focused on what he called "the most brutal, unremitting, non-stop violence ever filmed." Sadly, the reason as to why men would want to beat each other up, not for the desire to dominate but to participate, wasn't much discussed. In fact, the press was rather more interested in Brad's relationship with Jennifer Aniston than with *Fight Club*.

Of course, typical of Brad's choices, *Fight Club* was not the box office success the studio had hoped for. Art versus commerce was something Brad had to balance. As his salary climbs steadily, he feels pressure to prove his worth, and yet he is drawn consistently to films that are more artistic than commercial. And in some ways, that is understandable. *Fight Club* showed Brad at the height of his powers. It was far and away his best performance so far.

chapter 10

Back on Top

You know I've had this frustration with film because we can replicate feelings and, sometimes, a few of us get to an ultimate truth that when you witness it, it floors you because you weren't able to express it yourself... But my frustration with acting is that I can't do quite what music does. Music has its own language. It's not Japanese, it's not English, it's music.

Fight Club wrapped in December 1998, leaving Brad at loose ends. To him, this was not a bad thing. He had no work lined up, nothing on the backburner and nothing holding him down. He was unemployed, free to go with the flow—his favorite state of being. For the moment, he could focus on other important factors in his life: his family and his girlfriend, whom he brought together in August 1999. Sharing his blossoming interest in architecture, he drove his father around L.A. to look at several Frank Lloyd Wright originals in Hollywood hills. Such drives sparked conversation, and their conversations sparked action. Depressed about the universal strip-mall type of architecture so common in Springfield, Brad and his father embarked on a 50-house development project. Brad enthused, "We're going to do something where everybody's got space and light."

Before Brad's visit home, Brad and Jen, who was also on a break, took off to Europe to take in the architecture there. Their travels included Morocco, Portugal and Spain, where the paparazzi caught up with them, splashing photos of the couple throughout U.S. tabloids. While the couple was enjoying their European vacation, Brad learned he had been prey to an unexpected visitor—a stalker

"He won us all over. I read some rubbish printed about Brad, but I kept my opinions to myself until I met the geezer...He's as straightforward as they come."

had been arrested in his home. Like some twisted Goldilocks, 19-year-old Athena Rolando reportedly broke in and spent 10 hours wearing Brad's sweatpants and sleeping in his bed. Her stunt earned her much celebrity including TV appearances. As for the violation of his home and privacy, Brad said, "Who wants to hear me complain? What's the point? I don't have a say. It doesn't surprise me. It doesn't alarm me either. It's gross, and it's what I expect."

But stalkers aside, Brad was in great spirits. Struck by a new muse, he again began work on his 1910 Hollywood home. He had purchased surrounding properties, including a 1950s house. Now he had two houses to play with. He compared the way he thought when he was in a chaotic relationship to Wright's architecture—linear, proportional and strict. In his relationship with Jennifer, he found himself thinking more whimsically, responding more to clean lines and a modern perspective. Jennifer's influence brought warmth, because of her personal warmth and generosity, to his design work.

As for his other work, his career, Brad tried something a little different. He was so impressed with the British caper movie *Lock, Stock and Two Smoking Barrels,* that he called the director, Guy Ritchie, and asked if Ritchie had anything for him. Brad was clear that the size of the role or paycheck didn't matter: he just wanted to work with the director. It just so happened that Ritchie did have something in his next flick involving gypsies, pigs and diamonds. The role was Mickey O'Neill, the Irish Gypsy, and Brad played it with an indecipherable "Pikey" accent.

So, in December 1999, with Jen in tow, Brad went to London to make the movie *Snatch*. Ritchie and cast members were a little concerned how Hollywood's prettiest boy was going to fit in. These guys were blokes, after all, and not stars, but by all accounts, Brad became just another one of the lads. Vinnie Jones, ex-soccer player revered as much for his fighting as for his playing, said, "He won us all over. I read some rubbish printed about Brad, but I kept my opinions to myself until I met the geezer…He's as straightforward as they come." Brad didn't fit in only with the cast, however. He also fit into the movie beautifully, proving yet again that his talents come through in character, not leading, roles. His character, Mickey, isn't a starring role but he's the centre from which the three plots spin off and then come together for the resolution. Like Ritchie's debut, *Lock,*

Snatch (2000)

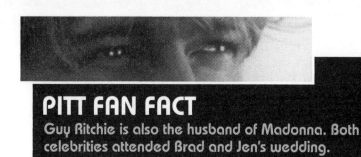

Stock and Two Smoking Barrels, Snatch explores the same criminal underworld of London. Stocked with over-the-top characters and situations and stylishly filmed, *Snatch* is a black comedy. Always conscious of pop culture, it smacks of irony and smarts.

Brad's next project was one that also stemmed mostly from his desire to play and little from his desire to advance his career. Friends since they both arrived in Hollywood as struggling actors, Brad and Julia Roberts had always wanted to work together, and in *The Mexican*, a three-hander quirky road movie, they got that chance. Gore Verbinski (*Mouse Hunt, Catch Me If You Can*) had been hired to direct the film for DreamWorks. Verbinski wasn't looking for an all-star cast as *The Mexican* was strictly low budget, but then David Fincher stepped in. Supportive of Verbrinski's developing career, Fincher called Brad and told him he should consider doing the film. Brad read the script, liked it, met with Verbinski, but it was Julia Roberts who really got things going. Brad's manager had sent Roberts the script. She liked it so much that she signed, and then Brad signed. Roberts suggested James Gandolfini as the third player, and he also signed.

"The fact that two working actors can both like a script mutually and find the time to do it and find a director that's brave enough to go there…It's no small miracle," Julia said about finally working with Brad. "This one came out of nowhere, and the idea of us jumping this kinda low-budget, gonzo, hit-and-run film just kind of appealed to us both," said Brad. Actually, Brad and Roberts shared little screen time together, as each of their characters is caught up in a different story line. The movie begins with Jerry, played by Brad, and Samantha, played by Roberts, together in a hotel room, but the couple soon starts bickering, which escalates to an all-out fight, and Samantha dumps Jerry's belongings from the balcony. Jerry, trying to go straight, has to do one more job for his criminal bosses: retrieve an antique gun from Mexico. Leroy, the hit man who wants to ensure that Jerry gets the gun, kidnaps Samantha. The total screen time Brad and Roberts share? Seven and one-half minutes.

It's interesting to note that these two movie stars who are of equal caliber and share a good friendship approach their work so differently. Verbinski observed, "There's a vast difference between Julia's working philosophy and Brad's. Brad's is a natural talent, and there's this intuitive thing that happens, something he nurtures, which is an enjoyable thing to watch blossom. He's willing to try anything. Julia is like a female Gene Hackman. She gets it right in two takes, and if you want something different, you'd better talk about it with her right then. She comes to play; she's on time. Don't call her to the set if you're not ready." Although Roberts won't ever be one of those laid-back actors—she does her homework— she appreciates those qualities in Brad, calling him "a very low-key, groovy guy." She went further to compliment his lack of complaining. "If I had to describe him in two

The Mexican (2001)

words," she said, "I'd say 'sunny disposition.' He radiates it to everyone around him."

Even with the biggest and brightest Hollywood pairing imaginable—Julia Roberts and Brad Pitt—on board, *The Mexican* retained its original, independent flavor, because this served the film's story line and themes. Unfortunately, the very starpower of their names undermined the essence of the film. Audiences turned out expecting a different movie, and they were angry when their expectations weren't met. This question—can a Hollywood star serve a low-budget art film well?—is something that Brad, with his penchant for the unusual, will have to look at. So far, Brad has starred only in mainstream movies, albeit, films that push the limits. But how many flops like *The Mexican* could Brad's career stand?

Brad's next project wasn't a movie, but it had a budget of a million dollars, super-secret logistics, seven months of planning and involved an A-list of stars. It was his wedding to Jen, announced on July 27, 2000, to take place at an undisclosed venue in two days' time. Finally, Brad's wish—to settle down, get married and have kids—was coming true, and he couldn't have found a more perfect woman. Jason Flemyng, who worked with Brad on *Snatch* and with Jen on *Rock Star*, said about spending time with the couple: "This will sound strange, but it was so nice to be around normal people. We just ate Mexican food and talked nonsense." He called Jen "a female Brad—couldn't be more gorgeous, yet utterly without vanity."

On Saturday July 29, 2000, 200 guests, friends, family and various stars arrived at the Malibu mansion of TV executive Marcy Carsey. Security was extremely tight: both guests and workers had to sign non-disclosure agreements. Since the St. Barts episode,

Marriage for Brad and Jennifer didn't change the nature of their nomadic lifestyles as actors.

Brad had become less tolerant and more paranoid of the paparazzi, and perceived his contact with them as a game. On his wedding day, he felt it was a game he should win. To prevent a circling of helicopters, the couple had approached the Federal Aviation Authority to see if they could clear the airspace around the house for the day, but they were refused. As they both wanted their wedding to take place on the beach, they decided they wouldn't let the paparazzi ruin this for them, although Jen had to prod Brad. "Jen finally said, 'Look, if they get the picture, they get it,' Brad admitted. 'Don't forget what this day is about.' She was right."

At 6:30 that evening, Jen walked down the aisle towards her husband-to-be, where they exchanged their personally written vows. Brad promised to "split the difference on the thermostat," and Jen promised to always make Brad's favorite milkshake. Although the promises were flip, the feelings were deep. Even Brad's nemesis respected the importance of the occasion: "At the very last minute, when the ceremony started, the press backed off. And I really have to thank them because they were just so cool. They let us have our moment, they let us have what turned out to be the highlight of my life."

Marriage for Brad and Jennifer didn't change the nature of their nomadic lifestyles as actors. Brad had signed up for two movies back to back, and Jen was busy with *Friends* and her own film career. "Distance is a beast," Brad said, echoing his feelings from his time with Juliette Lewis. But the couple had more ways to communicate now. First there was *Friends*, and as Brad said,

"Fortunately, you can find *Friends* in pretty much every country…I get to see *Friends* in Spanish or in German." Second, there was technology, and they could stay in touch through web cams.

Brad's next movie was a surprising choice: a leading role in a big-budget espionage thriller directed by Tony Scott, with whom Brad had worked with in *True Romance*, called *Spy Game*. Brad's dislike of the leading-man role was something he had often spoken about: "You know, the leading-man role, you could plug any of us in there. Cruise, Clooney, me. It's the same role. Because it's already been defined: the guy who can handle any situation. I understand why people want to see that. But there's no game in it for me."

Spy Game (2001)

But in the first movie since *Meet Joe Black*, *Spy Game* features Brad as the young romantic lead, Tom Bishop. His character, a rogue CIA agent, has been arrested in China for espionage and he will be executed if the U.S. government doesn't do something. Bishop was the one-time protégé of CIA operative Nathan Muir, now on the brink of retirement. Muir, aware the U.S. may have reasons not to help, takes on the mission to free Bishop. As he works towards his goal, Muir recalls how he recruited and trained the young rookie, at that time a sergeant in Vietnam, their troubled times together as operatives and the woman who threatened their friendship.

Robert Redford, playing the part of Muir, was probably the strongest influence on Brad's decision to play Bishop. Nine years after they had worked together on *A River Runs Through It*, they were reunited. However, this time, they would both be in front of the camera. But whatever Brad had hoped to get from working with Redford again, he seemed not to get. "It's really a father-son piece," Brad said of the movie, "although saying that makes me uncomfortable, and I'm sure it would make Bob even more uncomfortable." Reflecting on this further, he said, "I do think there's an older school where you don't show your feelings as much or your flaws—I see that with my father—but I also have to turn around and say Redford can be very sweet at times."

Reviews were positive, but box office results were tepid. One of the film's central questions asks how intelligence agencies fit in our post—cold-war era, a question that had suddenly become too relevant. Conceived long before the September 11 attacks on the U.S., the film had the misfortune of being released only two months after September 11. Audiences were not in the mood to watch a film with terrorism themes.

Ocean's Eleven (2001)

From one multi-million dollar film to another, Brad wrapped *Spy Game* and began *Ocean's Eleven*, a re-make of the Rat Pack caper flick, directed by Steven Soderbergh. Soderbergh had a golden reputation of making some of the best art movies in Hollywood. Recently, his reputation had spread, gaining him mainstream attention with *Erin Brockovich* and *Traffic*. With Soderbergh as director and George Clooney as ringmaster Danny Ocean reprising Frank Sinatra's role, finding an all-star cast to make up the rest of the gang wasn't difficult. Brad played Clooney's sidekick among a cast that included Matt Damon, Casey Affleck, Scott Cann, Don Cheadle, Carl Reiner, Andy Garcia and Julia Roberts.

> For Brad, a self-described loner and drifter, making **Ocean's Eleven** must have taken him back to his college years, living in a frat house. He was once again one of the guys, and not just any guys, but the really **cool** guys. Of Clooney, Brad said, "He's so easy to work with and bounce off of. He's great. Great laughs. It was like summer camp or a day off."

Ocean's Eleven wasn't meant to be anything more than smart, fun and very, very cool entertainment. Stylish, witty and packed with stars, *Ocean's Eleven* was an audience pleaser. Soderbergh, used to making more emotionally complex films, found the fluffiness hard to capture. "It's the hardest movie I've ever done. It's a movie about absolutely nothing, and I found it brain crushing. Everyday I felt I was hanging on by my fingernails."

We'll see where it goes....I find myself looking forward to a family.

Still, Soderbergh showed his gift yet again. For the first time since *Se7en*, Brad starred in a film that grossed over that $100 million mark.

But finishing *Ocean's Eleven* marked a new period of reflection for Brad. At 37, he was starting to question his longevity in the business. "On the one hand, I'm hitting my own stride now," he mused. "On the other hand, I'll tell you truthfully, I'm completely bored with myself in films. It's time for me to try either a new direction or new horizons. I have other interests that I want to pursue that mean more to me. I think there's room to go away from it for a while and then you can come back and re-invent. We'll see where it goes….I find myself looking forward to a family. It's not that I'm self-absorbed. Anything that's going to take the focus off myself, I welcome."

chapter 11

looking
Ahead

feel privileged. It means no more excuses, which I like. I just feel like I'm improved. I like the general label of "new and improved" or "old and improved," as the case may be. I'll trade that for the deterioration of the body, or whatever else that brings. I know it's impending.

—Brad, on turning 40

As fate would have it, the next two projects Brad planned to do fell through, and he ended up taking the next two years off. The time off, well deserved and needed, allowed Brad to process the recent changes in his life, most of all his marriage. And like the time off he took after *Fight Club*, Brad came back to public life more mature and more settled.

The press was insatiable for news of Brad and Jen. "Neither of us want to become the spokesman for happy marriage,

for 'coupledom,'" he said. "I'll tell you what I despise: this two-becomes-one thing where you lose your individuality. We don't cage each other with this pressure of happily ever after. You figure it out as you go along. We feel it out, rather than setting policies and rules. Jen and I always made a pact; that we'll see where this thing is going. I'm not sure it's really in our nature to be with someone for the rest of our lives, just because you made this pact. You keep going as long as you keep growing. When that dies, we do." Harsh as that may sound, it was Brad's way of being practical. Brad had learned to moderate his natural romantic self, because of his experiences, observations and values. On one hand, he valued marriage, but on the other, his experiences in prior relationships were hurtful, and Hollywood marriages were usually brief.

Still, he couldn't hide his love. "But it constantly surprises

Troy (2004)

me," he said, continuing his observation on his marriage. "Just when you think you've gotten all that you can out of it, you get knocked upside the head. It's good fun. We still have that friendship; we still have a good laugh, which can go in and out depending on the dynamics. It's complicated, but that's what keeps it interesting. We're good at getting s*** on the table. Then she tells other people, and I get mad," he joked.

His architectural and design work kept him occupied. It was time for the couple to find a home of their own. They purchased a French Normandy-style home in Beverly Hills. At the time, the home's major selling point for the couple was that it was in move-in shape. Then, Brad, being Brad, had it gutted. "I couldn't keep my hands off it," Brad grinned. The house was important to both Brad and Jen, particularly as they hoped to start a family; so creating an environment that brought together their different tastes made sense. And to Brad, Jen was the center of a home— literally and figuratively—"Her emphasis is the home, friends, and family. We all kind of crowd around her like moths to a flame. She's like a magnet; she brings a lot of people together that way. Jen's the fireplace that provides the warmth."

Jen had also given Brad the stability to resolve finally his two biggest issues: his pretty-boy image and his congenital sadness. The tension between being **People's** Sexiest Man of the Year and being a respected actor was not something Brad wanted to continue to create. Would the happiness he seeks always elude him? He began to embrace his sadness and find value in it.

Brad's hiatus also brought to him a new perspective on acting and a new acceptance. Gone was his usual self-deprecating view of himself. He had a whole new energy and verve to bring to his chosen career. After several years of feeling frustrated and disappointed, Brad realized he had a lot to offer as an actor: "I know what I'm after, what I have to offer. I'm more aware of what I can bring to a part, rather than another actor." It's a good thing that Brad was excited because when he began working again, with four back-to-back movies to shoot. Before starting these, however, he shot a cameo as a favor for friend George Clooney, who was directing his first movie, *Confessions of a Dangerous Mind*. His next movie was something new for Brad—he played a cartoon character, Sinbad, in *Sinbad: Legend of the Seven Seas*. He supplied the voice for the charming thief with a lot to learn about loyalty and women, and Brad enjoyed the experience very much. Directors Tim Johnson and Patrick Gilmore gave him the freedom he needed to play.

Next was the epic adventure *Troy*, in which Brad plays Homer's larger-than-life warrior, Achilles. For the first time, Brad took on the big box office action movie he'd spent his career avoiding. And Achilles is no slight hero, but a demigod who has existed for 3000 years, immortalized in Homer's *Iliad* as the ultimate warrior whose rage almost lost the Greeks the Trojan War. But as a true hero, Achilles accepted his fatal flaw and defeated Troy. "I finally caved," Brad said.

But Achilles is not a straight-ahead simple demigod, as director Wolfgang Peterson pointed out. Although it is a leading-man role, Achilles is hardly a hero. He may be beautiful and seem like a god, but he is also a hired killer with a dark soul. Stretching his acting skills, Brad had chosen yet another character with personal demons. *Troy* offered him a chance to play a complicated character, but it also extended an anti-war message, at least in Brad's interpretation. To Brad, *Troy* portrays "one civilization

> For the first time, Brad took on the big box office action movie he'd spent his career avoiding.

Ocean's Twelve (2004)

trying to overthrow another civilization." But Achilles' journey shows that "hatred of men is born; it dies." What is everlasting, Brad believes, is our humanity.

On the eve of his 40th birthday, Brad trained for five months to get in shape to play Achilles—five long months of weight training and sword fighting for an actor who is naturally blessed with a lean body and a dislike for exercise. He even quit smoking, although not for long. Then he was off to Malta and Mexico for five months of filming. Of Brad's heroic turn, respected co-star Peter O'Toole praised Brad for his preparation, authority, maturity, frankness, sensibility and vulnerability. "He's a good actor, and he's going to be a fine actor." High praise, indeed.

After the punishing physical shoot, Brad went to Italy to film *Mr. and Mrs. Smith*, a dark comedy about a bored married couple, each leading a secret life as an assassin. They are each other's next assignment. Co-starring Angelina Jolie, the film is slated for release in June 2005. Jolie explained that the movie is just a metaphor for marriage, and although the movie is a dark comedy, she assures moviegoers that the film is actually a positive, pro-marriage movie.

After wrapping *Mr. and Mrs. Smith*, Brad was reunited with the *Ocean's Eleven* gang for *Ocean's Twelve*, another kooky caper film. This time, the gang plans three heists in three countries, and Brad's character gets a little romance from an old flame played by Catherine Zeta Jones. From all accounts, the cast had

as much fun filming the sequel as they did *Ocean's Eleven*, and audiences should have as much fun as the first time around. After wrapping *Ocean's Twelve*, Brad had no more movie work lined up. He focused his attention on the production company he and Jen had formed, Plan B Productions. The company will release its first film in 2005: *Willie Wonka and the Chocolate Factory* starring Johnny Depp. Jen, however, has also been busy with several projects, also slated to appear in 2005, and she has several more in pre-production.

Brad has been exploring his Hollywood stardom in a new way. He organized a three-day architectural conference looking at the future of L.A.'s architecture. He has also become more politically active, supporting John Kerry in the 2004 Presidential Campaign, and advocating stem-cell research. In November 2004, Brad was appointed as a 46664 Ambassador. The 46664 campaign aims to raise awareness of the HIV/AIDS pandemic in South Africa. (The number 46664 was Nelson Mandela's prisoner's number while he was detained during the apartheid regime.) Finally, rather than just looking out onto the world, Brad is determined to be active about issues that touch him most deeply.

When he turned 40, Brad said, "I know there's a midlife crisis on its way. I'm sure there are some more rude awakenings yet to come. But I like it like that. I like the unknown." Brad was getting used to the ups and downs of his life. Good thing too, because he was right. Just a few weeks after his 41st birthday, the unbelievable happened.

Troy (2004)

On January 7, 2005, Brad and Jen issued a press release to *People* announcing they had separated after seven years. They gave no reason for their decision, just that they had thought about it carefully. They asked for the public's understanding and compassion during their difficult time. Sadly—and surprisingly—the "golden couple" was no more.

> **Just a month before their separation, Brad had told Diane Sawyer of his hopes for the future: "God, I'm finally going to say it: kids, family. I'm thinking family."**

So, what does the future have in store? Unfortunately, Brad's dreams of starting a family are on hold. At the end of March 2005, Jen filed for divorce, making the couple's reconciliation highly unlikely. We likely won't see much of Brad while he nurses his broken heart.

One thing is for sure: we'll be waiting for more headlines. No matter what, Brad Pitt is one of the most fascinating people in Hollywood. And no matter what, Brad will continue to grow, as a person and as an actor. He'll continue to take risks, and just when we think we have him figured out, he'll surprise us yet again. Stay tuned…

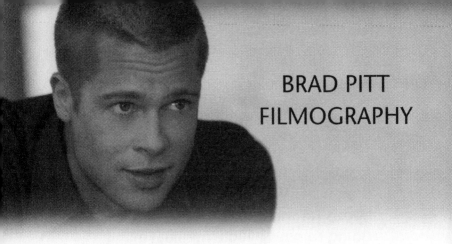

BRAD PITT FILMOGRAPHY

Mr. And Mrs. Smith (2005)

Ocean's Twelve (2004)

Troy (2004)

Sinbad: Legend of the Seven Seas (2004)

Confessions of a Dangerous Mind (2002)

Full Frontal (2002)

Ocean's Eleven (2001)

Spy Game (2001)

The Mexican (2001)

Snatch (2000)

Fight Club (1999)

Being John Malkovich (1999)

Meet Joe Black (1998)

Seven Years in Tibet (1997)

The Devil's Own (1997)

Sleepers (1996)

Twelve Monkeys (1995)

Se7en (1995)

Interview with the Vampire (1994)

Legends of the Fall (1994)

True Romance (1993)

Kalifornia (1993)

A River Runs Through It (1992)

Cool World (1992)

Johnny Suede (1991)

The Favor (1991)

Thelma and Louise (1991)

Across the Tracks (1991)

Happy Together (1989)

Cutting Class (1989)

TV Movies

Too Young to Die? (1990)

The Image (1989)

A Stoning in Fulham County (1988)

TV Series

Glory Days (1990)

Notes on Sources

Books

Robb, Brian J. *Brad Pitt: The Rise to Stardom*. London: Plexus, 2002.

Magazine Articles/Websites

http://pittcenter.com/index.htm

Angeli, M. "Born to be Brad." *Movieline Magazine*. (March 1993).

Bennett, L. "Aspects of Brad." *Vanity Fair Magazine*. (June 2004).

Biskind, P. "The Center of a Star." *Vanity Fair*. (December 2001).

Cooney, J. "Legends in the Making." *Empire Magazine*. (1994).

Dawson, J. "Drop Dead Gorgeous." *Empire Magazine*. (February 1999).

Dunn, J. "Rebel Star Top Dog." *Rolling Stone Magazine*. (April 1997).

Eds. "Brad Attitude: The World According to Mr. Pitt!" *Tiger Beat*. (March 1996).

Egan, M. "Brad to the Bone." *Details Magazine*. (January/February 2001).

Fernandez, J. "The Art of Being Brad." *USA Weekend*. (June 2001).

Forest, E. "The Esquire Interview." *Esquire Magazine UK Edition*. (September 2000).

Giles, J. "Brad Pitt's Cool World." *Details Magazine.* (August 1992).

Heath, C. "The Unbearable Bradness of Being." *Rolling Stone Magazine.* (October 1999).

Heller, Z. "Walking the Walk." *Harper's Bazaar Magazine.* (November 1998).

Horyn, C. "A Commanding Lead." *Vanity Fair Magazine.* (November 1998).

Mundy, C. "Slippin' Around on the Road with Brad Pitt." *Rolling Stone Magazine.* (December 1994).

Pearce, G. "Don't Look Down." *Empire Magazine.* (December 1997).

Reginato, J. "House of Brad." *W Magazine.* (October 2001).

Rynning, R. "Interview with the Vampire (and serial killer and cowboy loser and…)." *Sky Magazine.* (March 1994).

Schneller, J. "Brad Attitude." *Vanity Fair Magazine.* (February 1995).

Snowden, L. "Brad Pitt is Afraid of Sharks." *Premiere.* (October 1994).

Spines, C. "Brad Pitt: On Top of the World in Tibet." *Premiere UK Edition.* (December 1997).

Sventkey, B. "Blood Sweat and Fears." *Entertainment Weekly.* (October 1999).

Turner, J. "Not Half Brad." *Flaunt Magazine.* (December/January 2002).

Webber, B. "Oh Brad!" *Cleo Magazine.* (November 1992).

Detour Magazine. "Brad Influence." (April 1997).

TV Interviews

http://pittcenter.com/index.htm

Oprah, Harpo Productions. (November 1998 and May 3, 2004).

Primetime Live with Diane Sawyer, ABC. (August 10, 1997).

The Tonight Show with Jay Leno, NBC (January 2, 2001).

SOPHIE LEES

Born in London, England, Sophie has lived in Edmonton, Alberta, for much of her life. After training at the prestigious Studio 58 and earning an Honours degree in Drama from the University of Alberta, Sophie began her career as a local theatre actor and director. Best known for her work as the artistic director of Azimuth Theatre, she left theatre after 10 years. She tired of the constant search for funding, which stole more and more time from her creative work.

A recent graduate of the Professional Writing Program at Grant MacEwan College, Sophie is settling into her new career as a freelance writer and editor. One of her magazine articles, published in *AlbertaViews*, won a National and Western Magazine Award.

ICON
PRESS

STAR BIOGRAPHIES

Real stars. Real people. The life stories of show business celebrities as told by veteran entertainment reporters and industry insiders.

ORLANDO BLOOM: SHOOTING TO STARDOM

by Peter Boer

Hard to believe now perhaps, but when British actor Orlando Bloom appeared on the silver screen as Legolas in the first of the three *Lord of the Rings* films, he was a virtual unknown in the movie industry. In this readable biography, author Peter Boer details Bloom's rise to success, starting with his humble beginnings as a clay trapper at a Canterbury gun club. The book chronicles Bloom's progression through acting schools and colleges in London, as well as the back-breaking accident that changed the course of his life and propelled him on the path to stardom.

$7.95 USD/$9.95 CDN • ISBN 1-894864-18-2 • 5.25" x 8.25" • 144 pages

ANGELINA JOLIE: ANGEL IN DISGUISE

by Edrick Thay

The bee-stung lips. The vial of Billy Bob Thornton's blood. The notorious Oscar acceptance speech and the estrangement from her father, actor Jon Voight. Ever since she first entered the spotlight with her captivating and towering performance in HBO's *Gia*, Jolie's life and career have fascinated audiences.

$7.95 USD/$9.95 CDN • ISBN 1-894864-25-5 • 5.25" x 8.25" • 144 pages

JULIA ROBERTS: MORE THAN A PRETTY WOMAN

by Colin MacLean

Hollywood's highest paid actress is also a fascinating, complex woman who is already a legend. Entertainment journalist Colin MacLean uses personal interviews and in-depth research to find the enigmatic, intensely insecure but dedicated artist behind the famous megawatt smile.

$7.95 USD/$9.95 CDN • ISBN 1-894864-23-9 • 5.25" x 8.25" • 144 pages

RUSSELL CROWE: MAVERICK WITH A HEART

by Stone Wallace

Russell Crowe has displayed a versatility applauded by audiences and critics alike, from his notorious early role as the brutal skinhead Hando in *Romper Stomper* to his astounding portrayal as the brilliant but schizophrenic math genius John Nash in *A Beautiful Mind*. Crowe has been compared to many of the great stars of yesterday: Marlon Brando, James Dean, even Robert Mitchum and Spencer Tracy. As this highly readable biography shows, however, Crowe is very much his own man—onscreen and off.

$7.95 USD/$9.95 CDN • ISBN 1-894864-19-0 • 5.25" x 8.25" • 144 pages

SHANIA TWAIN: DENIM & DAZZLE

by Eva Marie Clarke

Shania Twain's 1995 album *The Woman in Me* launched her into the stratosphere of the country-pop music charts, eventually selling over 9 million copies in North America alone. This new biography by entertainment writer Eva Marie Clarke follows the rags-to-riches story of one of Canada's most famous musical exports.

$7.95 USD/$9.95 CDN • ISBN 1-894864-28-X • 5.25" x 8.25" • 144 pages

Look for books in the Star Biographies series at your local bookseller and newsstand or contact the distributor, Lone Pine Publishing, directly. In the U.S. call 1-800-518-3541. In Canada, call 1-800-661-9017.